D0342657

Praise for *Social Media Metrics*

"Jim has always been at the forefront of the Web analytics world. So, it makes perfect sense that he now tackles the complex world of figuring out Social Media. There are millions (probably billions) of conversations happening online. The big question becomes: what's a company to do? This book answers that question. How do you know if you're measuring the right parts of the program? Jim gets you downright dirty in the details."

—Mitch Joel, President, Twist Image, and Author
of *Six Pixels of Separation*

"For the better part of a decade, Jim Sterne has been advocating and explaining how to better understand the traffic coming to your web site. In fact he organized the largest organization of web analytics practitioners and companies with me: the Web Analytics Association. He also organized the most incredible conference on marketing optimization—the eMetrics Marketing Optimization Summit. This book belongs on every marketer's desk in this world of expanding digital marketing opportunities."

—Bryan Eisenberg, *New York Times* bestselling Author of *Waiting for Your Cat to Bark* and *Always Be Testing*

"It is entirely appropriate that the man who added clarity and definition to the topic of web metrics would be the same person to finally enlighten us about social media metrics. In *Web Metrics* Jim single-handedly paved the way for what has become a billion dollar industry, creating awareness where none previously existed. Now, with the publication of *Social Media Metrics* Jim has faced a more difficult challenge; mining through mountains of misinformation, disinformation, and flat out crap to provide the reader with nuggets of tangible, useful, and practical guidance.

—Eric T. Peterson, Author of *Web Analytics Demystified*

"This book will change the apparent chaos of social media into a measurable platform businesses can understand and benefit from."

—Alistair Croll and Sean Power, Authors of *Complete Web Monitoring* &
co-founders, Watching Websites

"This is one of those books that every marketer who has any role in planning social media will need to read, so you might as well sound smarter than everyone else and read it now."

—David Berkowitz, Senior Director of Emerging Media & Innovation, 360i

"For over 10 years, I've turned to Jim to regularly tell my audience about the latest trends in Web Analytics. He has an uncanny instinct for what is worth your time and attention and what isn't. His accessible and good-humored style will navigate you through this exciting and daunting field of Social Media Analytics."

—Larry Chase, Publisher, *Web Digest For Marketers*

"Since he won't say it himself, I'll say it for him. Jim Sterne is the godfather of Web metrics. He knows that often the need to measure something gets in the way of using that something effectively. Jim's clarity and wisdom distill a complex subject to its essence."
—Eric Ward, Content Linking Strategist aka LinkMoses

"Social media's ardent advocates all too often overlook a critical step: quantifying their efforts' impact. Sterne fills this void by providing a thorough explanation of different measurement approaches and tools, while underscoring how these metrics can improve social media programs and achieve business goals."
—Ellis Booker, Editor, *BtoB Magazine*

"Jim Sterne has been highly regarded as an online marketing thought leader for many years. And this long awaited new book sees him firmly established back at the top of the pile. Don't just talk about social media. Know social media. Measure social media. Be a master marketer in social media. Read this book."
—Mike Grehan, VP, Global Content Director,
Incisive Media, and Author of *Search Engine Marketing
(The Essential Best Practice Guide)*.

"This book is a must read for anyone investing in social media not just because it will help measure your success, but because it teaches you how to continuously improve your program."
—Katie Delahaye Paine, CEO, KDPaine & Partners

"Markets are conversations. People are your greatest asset. Customer centricity is the way forward. Social media is revolutionizing marketing. But how do you measure these things? How do you know how well you're doing? Jim Sterne, as ever, is the leading thinker and practitioner in answering these vitally important questions. Read his book. Heed his words."
—Ashley Friedlein, CEO, Econsultancy

"The Imperative: Use Jim Sterne's guidance to leapfrog your competitors with the simple fact that you must not only transform your media buys into social media programs (the new playing field); you must tie them to the three main goals of business—increased sales, lower costs, and improved customer satisfaction."
—Susan Bratton, CEO, Personal Life Media, Inc., and host
of the DishyMix show

"**Jim Sterne is a bold-faced liar.** This book is FAR more than he makes it out to be in his over-simplified introduction. It's *not* just about measuring the value of social media, but offers a clear roadmap to actually implementing an effective social media strategy. No one else explains it all so simply and common-sensically. Buy, borrow, or steal this book. Then protect it from office predators."
—Pat LaPointe, Managing Partner, MarketingNPV

"Jim is one of the foremost analytics experts in the world and he once again proves why. Not only does he identify the *how to measure* but also the value of the measures. This is one of those must reads that you actually must read—not may read. Jim knows more about this subject than anyone I know."
— Paul Greenberg, President, The 56 Group, and Author of *CRM at the Speed of Light*

"Jim Sterne continues to blaze new trails—the most incisive mind in web analytics now decodes social media. Get this excellent roadmap and start killing your competition!"
— Tim Ash, CEO of SiteTuners.com, and Author of *Landing Page Optimization*

"The first book I read on web measurement and analytics back in 2002 was *Web Metrics* by Jim Sterne. That book and the eMetrics Marketing Optimization Summit conference that followed defined a market and an industry. With Jim's pragmatic and commercially focused approach to understanding the impact of social media on your business this book will do the same again."
— Neil Mason, Director of Analytical Consulting, Foviance

"Social media is hot, but is it the right move for your business? Jim Sterne, the master of eMetrics, clearly explains in *Social Media Metrics* how to measure the business value of social media and track your success. Buy it when you're ready to move from social media hype to social media ROI."
— Bob Thompson, Founder and CEO, CustomerThink Corp.

"Jim Sterne steps outside of conventional thinking, offering readers a refreshing and useful methodology for thinking about the new ways that humans interact with brands and with each other. Addressing the niche between an obsession with 'number of followers' and mathematical theory, Mr. Sterne provides the business leader with holistic ways to strategically address this growing but often misunderstood channel."
— Kevin Hillstrom, President, MineThatData

"It's 'back to the future' with Jim's new book. A decade ago (or so) we built some of the first Web Analytic companies with names like—Net Genesis, Keylime, WebTrends, WebSideStory, and Ominiture who all had a vision in mind. Jim was the first expert to recognize and seize upon that vision—creating the seminal work which explains its value—and in so doing, an entire sector. A decade later, this new book does the same, only this time the outcomes are amplified as it involves us all in so many ways, and in every part of our life."
— Rand Schulman, Chief Marketing Officer, InsideView

"Not only does Jim close the gap between financial performance and social media engagement but he writes in a language that is universally understood by all marketing and business professionals. Jim never ceases to impress me with his ability to combine top notch education with engaging and entertaining content. Bottom line, you can't be in marketing and not have read this book."

—Aaron Kahlow, CEO, Online Marketing Institute

"This timely book unlocks the potential for optimal future budget allocation decisions to optimize business profitability."

—David Dalka, Marketing Change Management Strategist

"Jim's new book, *Social Media Metrics*, promises to be the capstone manuscript, pushing Social Media into the mainstream of business—past early adopters that have so far dominated this emerging field. *Social Media Metrics* is going to be the manual I give out to all my stakeholders and clients to read before they engage in Social Media."

—Marshall Sponder, Founder, Webmetricsguru.com

SOCIAL MEDIA METRICS

HOW TO MEASURE AND OPTIMIZE YOUR MARKETING INVESTMENT

JIM STERNE

WILEY

John Wiley & Sons, Inc.

Copyright © 2010 by Jim Sterne. All rights reserved.

Published by John Wiley & Sons, Inc., Hoboken, New Jersey.

Published simultaneously in Canada.

No part of this publication may be reproduced, stored in a retrieval system, or transmitted in any form or by any means, electronic, mechanical, photocopying, recording, scanning, or otherwise, except as permitted under Section 107 or 108 of the 1976 United States Copyright Act, without either the prior written permission of the Publisher, or authorization through payment of the appropriate per-copy fee to the Copyright Clearance Center, Inc., 222 Rosewood Drive, Danvers, MA 01923, (978) 750-8400, fax (978) 646-8600, or on the web at www.copyright.com. Requests to the Publisher for permission should be addressed to the Permissions Department, John Wiley & Sons, Inc., 111 River Street, Hoboken, NJ 07030, (201) 748-6011, fax (201) 748-6008, or online at http://www.wiley.com/go/permissions.

Limit of Liability/Disclaimer of Warranty: While the publisher and author have used their best efforts in preparing this book, they make no representations or warranties with respect to the accuracy or completeness of the contents of this book and specifically disclaim any implied warranties of merchantability or fitness for a particular purpose. No warranty may be created or extended by sales representatives or written sales materials. The advice and strategies contained herein may not be suitable for your situation. You should consult with a professional where appropriate. Neither the publisher nor author shall be liable for any loss of profit or any other commercial damages, including but not limited to special, incidental, consequential, or other damages.

For general information on our other products and services or for technical support, please contact our Customer Care Department within the United States at (800) 762-2974, outside the United States at (317) 572-3993 or fax (317) 572-4002.

Wiley also publishes its books in a variety of electronic formats. Some content that appears in print may not be available in electronic books. For more information about Wiley products, visit our web site at www.wiley.com.

Library of Congress Cataloging-in-Publication Data:

Sterne, Jim, 1955-
  Social media metrics : how to measure and optimize your marketing investment / by Jim Sterne.
    p. cm.
  Includes index.
  ISBN 978-0-470-58378-4 (cloth)
 1. Internet marketing. 2. Social media–Economic aspects. 3. Marketing research. 4. Online social networks–Economic aspects. I. Title.
  HF5415.1265.S7419 2010
  658.8'72–dc22

                                                              2010003833

Printed in the United States of America

10 9 8 7 6 5 4 3 2

Dedicated to Colleen

Contents

Foreword

A decade ago, I was vice president of marketing and PR for a NASDAQ-traded business-to-business technology company. We measured success in two ways. Our lead generation programs were measured via "sales leads": the number of people who requested a white paper or who tossed a business card into a fishbowl at the trade show. Our public relations programs were measured via a PR clip book, a gathering of all the clippings of magazine and newspaper articles written about the company. The book represented a month's worth of clippings and was usually bound for us by our PR agency.

Sales leads and press clips were very common forms of measurement accepted by management in many B2B companies. Success—or failure—at a trade show was based on the number of people who stopped by the booth. And in a good month, our PR agency would proudly drop the clip book on a table to hear the "thud factor." A deep, resonating boom was very, very good indeed.

Fast forward to 2010. Social media gives everyone—not only B2B companies but also consumer brands, consultants, nonprofits, and even rock bands, churches, and colleges—a tremendous opportunity to reach people and engage them in new and different ways. Now we can earn attention by creating something interesting and valuable and then publishing it online for free: a YouTube video, a blog, a research report, photos, a Twitter stream, an e-book, a Facebook page.

Those measurements, which seemed so great in an offline world, are wholly inadequate online. But what should we do instead? A debate has raged in recent years. On one hand, people tried to adapt old (but successful) offline measurements to the social media world. For example, many marketers slapped registration pages onto practically all content, generating "leads" but preventing people from sharing. On the other hand, a cadre of social media proponents argued for no measurement at all, since "social media is just different." I'll admit that I too was stumped, and yet at nearly every speech I give, somebody asked about measurement.

Fortunately, Jim Sterne came to the rescue with this terrific book.

In fact, when Wiley approached me to work on *The New Rules of Social Media* book series, the only book I *knew* I had to have was one on measurement. And the only person to write it was Jim. As founder and organizer of the eMetrics Marketing Optimization Summits (held in ten cities around the world each year), Jim is the undisputed leader in online marketing metrics. He is scary smart about measuring and optimizing marketing investment in social media. As I read the manuscript that became this book, I learned something on every page.

Whether you are selling online, through a direct sales force, or via distribution channels, social media is a critical part of the mix. But you know that already. If you're like I was, what you don't know yet is how to measure and—when actually armed with that data—how to improve.

I particularly like that *Social Media Metrics* is crammed with examples from real-world companies for you to learn from. Far from an academic tome on regression analysis, this is a practical book packed with ideas you can apply to your business today.

Of course, while you'll learn what to measure, how to do it, and how to act on your results, what Jim is really teaching you in these pages is how to be successful. Armed with the metrics and strategies you need to reach your audiences, you'll be ready to help your business prosper.

Now you've got no excuses! Start building your social media marketing machine now; Jim will teach you exactly how to measure success.

— David Meerman Scott
Businessweek bestselling author of
The New Rules of Marketing & PR
www.WebInkNow.com
twitter.com/dmscott

Acknowledgments

Living in a socially connected world, I find myself beholden to more people than I can say and many more who have no idea how much they helped me. But I am pleased to list a few who have been influential, inspirational, informative, and supportive, whether they knew it or not. My thanks to:

Akin Arikan, Anil Batra, Shanee Ben-Zur, Susan Bratton, Vicky Brock, Chris Brogan, Joseph Carrabis, Pete Cashmore, Larry Chase, Barbara Coll, Alistair Croll, René Dechamps Otamendi, Laura Lee Dooley, Rick Eagle, Bryan Eisenberg, Steve Ennen, Ashley Friedlein, Mark Gibbs, Seth Godin, Mike Grehan, Andrea Hadley, Josh Hallett, Stéphane Hamel, Shel Israel, Mitch Joel, Beth Kanter, Avinash Kaushik, Vida Killian, Matthew Lange, Alex Langshur, Charlene Li, June Li, Rebecca Lieb, Dylan Lewis, Neil Mason, Jodi McDermott, John McKean, Lisa Morgan, Dennis Mortensen, Jim Novo, Jeremiah Owyang, Katie Paine, Bob Page, Eric Peterson, Sean Power, Jack Powers, David Rhee, Howard Rheingold, Robert Scoble, David Meerman Scott, Rachel Scotto, Peter Shankman, Philip Sheldrake, Crispin Sheraden, Rand Schulman, Marshall Sponder, Karl Sterne, Suresh Vittal, Daniel Waisberg, and Ed Wu.

Introduction: Getting Started—Understanding the Ground Rules

When you pick up a book in a bookstore or "look inside" online, you want the briefest, clearest, most meaningful description of the content you can get, along with a feel for the writing style. Allow me to help:

This Book Is About	This Book Is Not About
Measuring the business value of social media	Measuring social media's size and popularity
Measuring the importance of social media to organizations	Measuring the importance of social media to mankind
Making the most of social media for business in a community-acceptable, brand enhancing way	Auto-posting and auto-tweeting your make-money-fast message in a scorched-earth marketing way
How to gauge the value of your social media efforts	How to *do* social media really well

Why? Because:

While much has been written questioning the value of social media, this landmark study has found that the most valuable brands in the world are experiencing a direct correlation between top financial performance and deep social media engagement. The relationship is apparent and significant: Socially engaged companies are in fact more financially successful.

—ENGAGEMENTdb: Ranking the Top 100 Global Brands

Social Media Defined

The Internet has always been a social medium. It is unique because it is the first many-to-many communication channel. The telephone is one-to-one. Broadcast is one-to-many. The Internet is so unique because it has always been all about the average Joe being able to communicate with the rest of the world.

It started when bulletin board systems gave up their direct modem banks and became newsgroups. The ability to post and respond expanded beyond those who knew the code (the telephone number). As e-mail became more ubiquitous, discussion lists sprang up and never went away. Next, people learned how to build web sites. It was cheap and required neither a permit nor an advanced degree. It was the "great playing field leveler," allowing David to square off against the media-controlling Goliath.

Blogging melded together the power of the conversation with a giant leap forward in ease of use. Flickr and YouTube made uploading pictures and videos a snap. Then Twitter made opt-in, instant messaging so simple, it couldn't help but catch fire. A perfect storm. What was always a hyper-drive communication tool became a nuclear-powered communication tool on steroids.

For the purposes of this book, "social media" is that which allows anybody to communicate with everybody. In other words, consumer-generated content distributed through easy-to-access online tools.

Is this out-of-control capability that has people uploading pictures of their lunch really useful to business? Oh yes.

How valuable? Ahhh . . . That is an excellent question.

SOCIAL MEDIA CATALOG

There are six broad categories of social media and probably two more before this book hits the streets.

Forums and Message Boards

These range from the old newsgroups to threaded discussion groups where people can submit a question or an opinion and others can offer up an answer or an attitude. These can happen through e-mail only or can be hosted privately, semi-privately, or publicly. Companies can host their own to closely monitor the conversation.

Review and Opinion Sites

Amazon.com has allowed customers to comment on books and goods for years. Epinions.com started last century (May 1999) as the place where buyers could discuss the ins and outs of products they love and hate without being pummeled by the vendors who were trying to sell them things. Now, thanks to syndication services like Bazaarvoice, most ecommerce sites have a place for the voice of the customer.

Social Networks

MySpace, LinkedIn, and Facebook are semi-open communities for connecting online. Sites like Ning allow anybody to create an open or closed group for communication, collaboration, and through-a-friend connection. Social games are slotted into this category but are not delved into here.

Blogging

Blogs made posting your opinion to the world so easy that everybody can publish their opinion. Organizations can promote their perspective on the one hand and everybody can talk about how lame they are on personal blogs. This dichotomy splits the metrics between measuring how well you are communicating and how others are talking about you.

Microblogging

Twitter, microblogging poster child. Everything frm love testimonials 2 divorce announcements in 140 characters or less—even frm yr phone.

Bookmarking

Digg, Delicious, and Stumbleupon let individuals tell the world what they think is cool, important, useful, interesting, etc. Showing up on the home page of these can skyrocket your traffic.

Media Sharing

I grew up in a house with a slide projector and a screen in the hall closet. Friends, family, neighbors, and dates were subjected to the latest vacation, trip to the beach, or art walk. Now that Flickr puts all our photos a click away and YouTube hosts all our videos, I miss those communal times of storytelling. I'm looking forward to digital projectors or large-format TV monitors dropping in price enough to have one in every home.

In the meantime, online media sharing isn't about showing your dinner party your snapshots; it's about showing the world your snaps and videos and allowing the world to comment. This is where virality got serious.

Social Media Is a Given

Word of mouth is the number one influence on the decision to buy a car . . . Social media democratizes providing word of mouth to a much broader audience.

— Fritz Henderson, CEO, General Motors in
interview with David Meerman Scott,
September 2009

Whether you are selling online, through a direct sales force, or through distribution channels, what people are saying about you online is now more important than your advertising. Social media is no longer a curiosity on the horizon but a significant part of your marketing mix. We accept these truths as self-evident at the start of this book so we can get right to the discussion of measurement.

I will forgo the chest beating about how social media is the Medium of the Masses or the Solution to All of Man's Ills. Many others have gone to great lengths to convince you and they are right, but their points need not be belabored here. If you're still not sure whether social media is important or is important to your company, save this book for later. After you've read some of the hundreds of books, thousands of blogs, or millions of tweets and are convinced, it'll be time to come back here for a review of measuring the use of these tools for business.

100 WAYS TO MEASURE SOCIAL MEDIA

For those of you in a hurry to grab a list of metrics, this is it. David Berkowitz has taken the time to save you the trouble and his "100 Ways to Measure Social Media" was posted on his Inside the Marketers Studio blog (www.marketersstudio .com/2009/11/100-ways-to-measure-social-media-.html). If it's metrics you're after, here they are and you need read no further than David's list:

1. Volume of consumer-created buzz for a brand based on number of posts

2. Amount of buzz based on number of impressions

3. Shift in buzz over time

4. Buzz by time of day/daypart

5. Seasonality of buzz

6. Competitive buzz

7. Buzz by category/topic

8. Buzz by social channel (forums, social networks, blogs, Twitter, etc.)

9. Buzz by stage in purchase funnel (e.g., researching vs. completing transaction vs. post-purchase)

10. Asset popularity (e.g., if several videos are available to embed, which is used more)

11. Mainstream media mentions

12. Fans

13. Followers

14. Friends

15. Growth rate of fans, followers, and friends

16. Rate of virality/pass-along

17. Change in virality rates over time

18. Second-degree reach (connections to fans, followers, and friends exposed—by people or impressions)

19. Embeds/Installs

20. Downloads

21. Uploads

22. User-initiated views (e.g., for videos)

23. Ratio of embeds or favoriting to views

24. Likes/favorites

25. Comments

26. Ratings

27. Social bookmarks

28. Subscriptions (RSS, podcasts, video series)

29. Pageviews (for blogs, microsites, etc.)

30. Effective CPM based on spend per impressions received

31. Change in search engine rankings for the site linked to through social media

32. Change in search engine share of voice for all social sites promoting the brand

33. Increase in searches due to social activity

34. Percentage of buzz containing links

35. Links ranked by influence of publishers

36. Percentage of buzz containing multimedia (images, video, audio)

37. Share of voice on social sites when running earned and paid media in same environment

38. Influence of consumers reached

39. Influence of publishers reached (e.g., blogs)

40. Influence of brands participating in social channels

41. Demographics of target audience engaged with social channels

42. Demographics of audience reached through social media

43. Social media habits/interests of target audience

44. Geography of participating consumers

45. Sentiment by volume of posts

46. Sentiment by volume of impressions

47. Shift in sentiment before, during, and after social marketing programs

48. Languages spoken by participating consumers

49. Time spent with distributed content

50. Time spent on site through social media referrals

51. Method of content discovery (search, pass-along, discovery engines, etc.)

52. Clicks

53. Percentage of traffic generated from earned media

54. View-throughs

55. Number of interactions

56. Interaction/engagement rate

57. Frequency of social interactions per consumer

58. Percentage of videos viewed

59. Polls taken/votes received

60. Brand association

61. Purchase consideration

62. Number of user-generated submissions received

63. Exposures of virtual gifts

64. Number of virtual gifts given

65. Relative popularity of content

66. Tags added

67. Attributes of tags (e.g., how well they match the brand's perception of itself)

68. Registrations from third-party social logins (e.g., Facebook Connect, Twitter OAuth)

69. Registrations by channel (e.g., Web, desktop application, mobile application, SMS, etc.)

70. Contest entries

71. Number of chat room participants

72. Wiki contributors

73. Impact of offline marketing/events on social marketing programs or buzz

74. User-generated content created that can be used by the marketer in other channels

75. Customers assisted

76. Savings per customer assisted through direct social media interactions compared to other channels (e.g., call centers, in-store)

77. Savings generated by enabling customers to connect with each other

78. Impact on first contact resolution (FCR) (hat tip to Forrester Research for that one)

79. Customer satisfaction

80. Volume of customer feedback generated

81. Research & development time saved based on feedback from social media

82. Suggestions implemented from social feedback

83. Costs saved from not spending on traditional research

84. Impact on online sales

85. Impact on offline sales

86. Discount redemption rate

87. Impact on other offline behavior (e.g., TV tune-in)

88. Leads generated

89. Products sampled

90. Visits to store locator pages

91. Conversion change due to user ratings, reviews

92. Rate of customer/visitor retention

93. Impact on customer lifetime value

94. Customer acquisition/retention costs through social media

95. Change in market share

96. Earned media's impact on results from paid media

97. Responses to socially posted events

98. Attendance generated at in-person events

99. Employees reached (for internal programs)

100. Job applications received

Happy now? Good. If, on the other hand, you actually want to know if any of these metrics are useful and how to use them then you'll need to heed David's advice: "Ultimately, you need to start with figuring out your business objectives and then apply these metrics accordingly."

This Book Is for Business People

This book is for marketers who already *know* that social media is important and want to get a better handle on managing it as a serious business tool.

This book is for senior executives who want to take the step from merely understanding social media to managing social media as a real corporate asset rather than tolerating it as the latest cool online fad.

This book is for marketing managers who are still looking for ways to convince upper management to invest resources in social media. They are looking for corroboration and validation.

This book is for junior marketers who have been handed social media as yet another assignment and are tasked with bringing in results. They are on the hook for making solid business decisions about budget allocation and need a way to demonstrate the value of their efforts. They need an ally in their struggle to petition for appropriate resources.

This book is for small business people who are looking for any way to engage prospective customers at the lowest cost possible.

This book is for university professors who need to explain the practical value of social media to their very media savvy students while teaching them marketing.

This book is for advertising agencies, web marketing companies, and social media consultants as they strive to help their clients live up to customer expectations.

If you were hoping for a book on how to blog, tweet, post, digg, befriend, or follow, this ain't it. But it will tell you how to determine if you are doing any of those things well.

A shift in philosophy, a modification in strategy, and brand-new metrics are the keys to marketing success in an interconnected world. Other books will explain why social media is critical and how to go about participating. This book is focused on measuring the success of your social media marketing efforts.

How This Book Is Organized

Chapter 1: Getting Focused—Identifying Goals

Why are you even bothering with social media? If you don't know, you do not want to step in blindly. This is the realm of public opinion and customer conversations. You do not want to blunder onto the scene without a clear idea of why you are there and what you want out of it. Not only are you sure to make hash of it, anything you measure will be context free and worse than useless.

The Big Three Goals in business are:

1. Increased Revenue,

2. Lowered Costs, and

3. Improved Customer Satisfaction

They are all that matters in the long run. If the work you do does not result in an uptick in one or more of those Big Three Goals, then you are wasting your time and spinning your wheels.

There are a myriad of factors that indicate whether you are attaining one or more of these Big Three Goals. You need to keep an eye on these critical factors because you are running your marketing programs in real time and can't wait for month-end or quarterly results to make adjustments along the way. "Are we there yet?" is the wrong question. "Are we still going in the right direction?" is the question that leads to business and career success.

Chapter 2: Getting Attention—Reaching Your Audience

Measuring message delivery in social media is a lot like measuring it in classic advertising venues, so classic metrics apply. Awareness, reach, and frequency are necessary to determine if your message is getting out there. Yes, there's a twist.

You've reached a large number of people. That's great! But it's a small part of the story. Success in social media is not found in how many people got your message; it's found in how many people thought your message was remarkable—literally. How many people were intrigued enough by the point you were making to comment on it and pass it along to their friends?

This is word of mouth like you've never seen before, so be prepared to deal with a yardstick that has become articulated and multidimensional.

Chapter 3: Getting Respect—Identifying Influence

Social network node graphing was a fascinating theoretical pastime until the Internet came along and allowed us to actually map the connections. The marketer's task now includes understanding the impact of reaching the people who are communication nodes.

When a tree falls in a forest and there is nobody there to hear it, it makes no difference whether it makes a sound or not. If a leaf falls in a forest and there are thousands standing within earshot, the effect is so small, it make no difference.

Posting a brilliant insight to a blog that has no readers or tweeting something so banal that it has no retweeters is just as useless. Your message multiplier velocity and reach are the signals that tell you whether your insight is popular or prosaic.

Your message multiplier tells you how many people thought your message was worthy of repeating, how quickly the message spread, and the scope of its dissemination. These are essential measures for determining whether you are resonating with your target audience and who within your organization is best equipped to be the face of the firm in the social media spheres. Influencity, anybody?

Chapter 4: Getting Emotional—Recognizing the Sentiment

Counting is fine but now we can detect opinion.

There have long been text analysis tools that focused on unstructured data like documents, spreadsheets, and survey results. Used primarily as search tools, they are being trained on the ocean of emotion called the social media space.

Analyzing the outpouring of millions of souls can reveal attitudinal shifts that are not visible to opinion polls, survey takers, or customer satisfaction questionnaires. Tracking public sentiment over time provides invaluable insight and gives you the chance to stay right on top of changes in the marketplace and your organization's brand equity.

Chapter 5: Getting Response—Triggering Action

If they read it, repeat it, and like it a lot, you're only part of the way home.

Tracking the variations in brand affection in the hearts and minds of the public is important, but measuring the results your social media efforts engender is vital.

Do people click through to your web site based on their social media interactions? Do they engage with your organization in new and different ways? Are more people drawn into a profitable and sustainable relationship with your company? Tracking the actions that result from all your blogging, tweeting, and YouTubing is where the money is.

Chapter 6: Getting the Message—Hearing the Conversation

Getting the right message to the right person at the right time has been the hallmark of great advertisers and marketers over the years. But with the customer in control, you want to make sure you are measuring your ability to get the right message from the right people at the right time.

Social media has become the Great Market Research System. It allows you to eavesdrop on your marketplace and find out what your target audience is thinking and feeling. You can incorporate that knowledge into your marketing mix, you can make it a fundamental part of your customer service and support and you can feed it directly into your business strategy planning.

Measuring how well you hear is much different from measuring how well you speak or sing or shout.

Chapter 7: Getting Results—Driving Business Outcomes

You're measuring what sort of response you're getting. Now it's time to cycle back around to measuring what sort of business impact your efforts are having.

Whether you employ an intern, use a spreadsheet, or even just glance at a dashboard, social media is not going to do any good for your company unless you can tell if the results are an increase in revenue, a lowering of costs, and/or an improvement in customer satisfaction.

With your new insights about how social media really works, it's time to reexamine your goals. The Big Three will certainly stand the test of time, but your Key Performance Indicators are sure to need a reevaluation.

Chapter 8: Getting Buy-In—Convincing Your Colleagues

Senior managers are not dumb, but they are slow to understand and embrace new communications methods.

Chances are excellent that your boss and his boss and her boss did not grow up with Internet access. Maybe they didn't even have it at college. You need to take some steps to convince them that social media is not only inevitable and not only a vital part of your marketing mix, but is a pathway to profits and it deserves the resources to be properly measured.

Chapter 9: Getting Ahead—Seeing the Future

What does social media look like in two or ten years? How do you measure this strange and wonderful world of actually talking to people in public as it constantly changes?

There are some changes coming that seem inevitable and some that will take us all by surprise. Looking into the crystal ball is always entertaining—and a little nerve wracking.

One thing we know for certain. As far into the future as you care to look, you will still need to measure your efforts against your goals. You gotta have goals.

Let's start there, shall we?

CHAPTER 1
Getting Focused—Identifying Goals

I know the price of success: dedication, hard work, and an unremitting devotion to the things you want to see happen.

— Frank Lloyd Wright

Give me a stock clerk with a goal and I'll give you a man who will make history. Give me a man with no goals and I'll give you a stock clerk.

—J.C. Penney

Measuring for measurement's sake is a fool's errand. But we're all fools now and again.

The human mind loves order. People think their iPod really knows how they feel by how it sequences songs just so when set to "shuffle." People tell fortunes by reading the leaves in the bottom of a tea cup or from the succession of upturned tarot cards. When faced with absolute randomness, the human mind kicks into overdrive to find patterns. We enjoy spending quiet time on the grass finding animals in the clouds, and conspiracy theorists can find plots and schemes in random events.

In the same way, web marketers have attempted to divine significance from the rows of IP addresses, file names, byte counts, and time stamps in the log files of web servers from the very beginning.

Over the years, with the advent of additional data collection technologies, we have proven that our conjectures and prognostications are valuable to business. Hypotheses can be scientifically tested to show that we understand and can influence onsite behavior by making specific changes to a web site and measuring the results. We can alter our prospective customers' behavior by altering our promotional efforts and persuasion techniques.

Measurement Is No Longer Optional

Katie Delahaye Paine is a PR maven who understands social media better than most. She's an insightful consultant and an engaging speaker, and one of her more popular PowerPoint presentations is available online at www.themeasurementstandard.com/issues/5-1-09/paine7stepssocial5-1-09.asp. It's called "7 Steps to Measurable Social Media Success."

In step two, Katie advocates setting clear, measurable objectives. She says you need to know what problem you need to solve, you need to not do anything in social media if it doesn't add value, and she reminds us that you can't manage what you can't measure—so set measurable goals.

Whether money is tight or times are good, everybody is bent on improving their business performance based on metrics. You cannot continue to fly by the seat of your pants. Automated systems and navigational instrumentation are required on passenger planes, and your business deserves no less.

As the tools escalate in sophistication, there remains one truism that cannot be ignored. Regardless of the amount of data and the cleverness of analytics tools one has, we still need analysis. The sharpest analyst or most talented statistician in the world is stymied without data, to be sure. But without those brilliant minds cogitating about a given purpose, those tools and data can create pretty charts and graphs and not much else. The most frequent missing piece is a specific problem to solve.

Every analyst has been asked to describe the past, explain the present, and tell the future given a data warehouse full of bits and bytes and the assumed ability to interpret human intent.

When faced with the question "Here's a bunch of data—what does it mean?" there are only two responses. The first is a tedious explanation of how the word "data" is the plural of datum and therefore the inquisitor's grammar is lacking. This approach is tiresome for the addressee and only fun for the analyst the first couple of times. The second response is "What problem are we solving for?" While this is an equally egregious mangling of the King's English, it is an integral part of the analytical vernacular.

The question, while sounding just as haughty as the former grammar lesson, is critical. When getting into a taxi, one is expected to know and communicate one's destination. Of course a statistician can groom a large data dump and find correlations between temperature, elevation, and the rate of change in barometric pressure. But he won't volunteer the critical answer of whether you should bring an umbrella unless you specifically ask, "Do you think it might rain?"

The same is true of marketing—especially online marketing—where we are data rich and insight poor.

Measurement, Metrics, and Key Performance Indicators

There were 4,231 views and mentions of your viral marketing campaign on the first day.

On hearing this, you might jump out of your chair, run down the hall, high-five the older members of your team, fist-bump the younger ones, and open a bottle of champagne. Alternatively, you might slump in your chair, hide from the rest of your team, and open a bottle of antidepressants.

Four thousand two hundred and thirty-one is a measurement. Without context, it is merely a number. When compared with your personal best, company expectations, or your competitors' efforts, that number becomes a metric. It is now indicative of value, importance, or a change in results.

If that metric is central to the well-being of the organization, it might be considered a Key Performance Indicator (KPI). It might be worthy of daily e-mail updates, dashboard placement, and iPhone App notifications. To be a KPI, it must indicate how well your organization's goals are being served. Therein lies the rub—the downfall of web measurement people everywhere: ill-defined objectives.

Without context, your measurements are meaningless.

Without specific business goals, your metrics are meaningless.

Proceed Ye No Further if Ye Have No Goals

It is crucial to map out your specific business goals before embarking on a social media program. As Yogi Berra put it, "If you don't know where you are going, you will wind up somewhere else."

Companies that tout their "success" because they track the number of friends and followers will never compete effectively with those who track sales and profits gained from reaching out to their followers. You want a goal? Income's a great goal—but it's not alone.

THE BIG THREE BUSINESS GOALS

It's time to get very high-level. There are only three true business goals (Figure 1.1).

They are all that matters in the long run. If the work you do does not result in an improvement to one or more of these Big Three Goals, then you are wasting your time, wasting money, spinning your wheels, alienating customers, and not helping the organization. You may be covering your backside and building your empire, but in the long run you will not ensure your status as an employee.

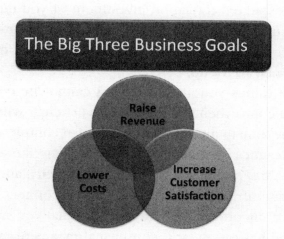

Figure 1.1 Your focus should always be on either increasing revenue, lowering costs, or improving customer satisfaction. Doing all three would be just fine.

There are many measurable elements that indicate whether you are improving on one or more of these Big Three Goals. You need to keep an eye on these critical factors because you are running your marketing programs in real time and can't wait for month-end or quarterly results to make adjustments along the way. "Are we there yet?" is the question asked from the backseat. "Are we still going in the right direction?" and "Is there anything in the way?" are asked from behind the wheel and lead to business and career success.

You can always think of something to earn more, spend less, and make customers happier. If you can do all three at the same time, do please give me a call. You are headed for greatness, and I love a good case study.

Increased Revenue

Considered the easiest to measure, revenue is always tabulated in terms of cash. You raked it in or you didn't. You met the expected return on investment or you missed the mark. You brought in more this time than last time or you fell under the bus. A Mark, a Yen, a Buck or a Pound, they are very easy to tot up.

If the things you are measuring cannot be connected back to income, then you need to be very clear why you are taking the time to measure them. You can completely baffle your colleagues with analytics colloquialisms like sentiment volatility rate, pass-along engagement velocity, and uptake-to-captivation ratios. But as soon as you connect the dots to arrive at income, everybody knows what you are talking about and has a standard, consensual means of evaluating the righteousness of your social marketing programs.

While income is always the pot of gold at the end of the rainbow, there is another consideration that cannot be ignored: the other side of the profit equation called Cost.

Lowered Costs

It's easy to bring in a million dollars; just sell two million one-dollar bills for 50 cents each. Clearly, your attention should be focused on profits. So, while coming up with new and innovative ways to make sales, don't forget to come up with new and innovative ways to lower expenses. If you can lower the cost of finding that pot of gold, then there's more net gold to go around.

Customer service and market research are the obvious areas where social media can boost profits by lowering costs, but it's a fine balance. You must spend money to make money, but if you can show that social media is a less expensive way to measure public opinion, make friends, and influence people, then you can have a larger share of the budget next time around. Oh, and you get to keep your job, too.

Improved Customer Satisfaction

The great thing about improving customer satisfaction is that it raises revenue and lowers cost. Happier customers are more likely to buy again. It is cheaper to sell something to somebody already in your database than it is to have to beat the bushes to find new ones. So if customer satisfaction is a factor in income and expense, and if income and expense are simply part of the profit equation, then the only goal worth worrying about is profits, right? Not so fast, Mr. Lay.

Remember Kenneth Lay? The famous CEO, last seen being walked out of Enron headquarters wearing government-issued bracelets? It seems that when one focuses on profits alone, one steps in over one's head with unpleasant results.

Happy customers are necessary to the life of a business if you can just force yourself to look beyond the quarterly report. A 6- or 9- or 12-month window will verify that a company with unhappy customers is not on a path to survival. Curiously, there is proof. A company's American Customer Satisfaction Index score "has been shown to be predictive of both consumer spending and stock market growth, among other important indicators of economic growth" (www.theacsi.org). Yes, that's right, happier customers make for increased stock prices.

THE FREE CALCULATOR DILEMMA

If you need a down and dirty answer to how much social media can raise revenue and lower costs, there are plenty of online tools like DragonSearch's Social Networking Media ROI Calculator (Figure 1.2). These calculations are ideal for those who have to fit into a specific budget and wish to manipulate the numbers until they do what they're told.

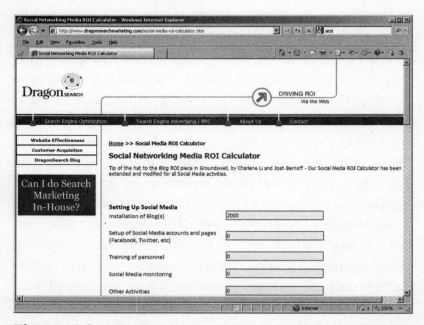

Figure 1.2 DragonSearch's Social Networking Media ROI Calculator lets you fudge the numbers till they'll play nice. (www .dragonsearchmarketing.com/social-media-roi-calculator.htm)

All spreadsheets can help in the same way. You can play what-if until the cows come home or at least until the boss allocates another sliver of the budget for a Facebook app that might go viral.

The solution is to get a clear handle on your goals and sweep up a handful of online metrics tools and services to prove your point. Show the actual results of your endeavors rather than hockey-stick conjectures. Just don't go overboard. That'll lead you to where the tool-price quandary pendulum swings too far the other way.

THE EXPENSIVE CALCULATOR DILEMMA

With a decent calculator, you can add, subtract, multiply, divide, and get on about your business. With a spreadsheet, you can play what-if scenarios until your keyboard wears out. With a customer relationship management system, a dynamic content management server, an integrated ad server, a recommendation engine, and a sentiment analysis system, you can deliver the right message to the right person at the right time. And, given a supercomputer the size of Deep Thought, you can calculate the answer to life, the universe, and everything—in about 7½ million years. But should you?

If that spreadsheet has enough horsepower for the project, you do not want to spend more than you can get in return. Here's where calculating the ROI on ROI rears its ugly head.

Suppose you used a million dollars' worth of the world's most sophisticated tools to increase sales by .002 percent. Not something you'd want in your LinkedIn profile. Unless, of course, you thereby delivered an additional $7.5 million in sales. Update LinkedIn, Facebook, and MySpace and reach for the champagne bottle. Kudos to you and well worth the price for all those tools. If you don't happen to work for Walmart and your organization doesn't happen to sell $375 billion in goods every year, then your mileage, online self-aggrandizement, and bottle choice may vary.

The most important part of all analysis is whether and how the resulting metrics will be used. If you want to know how many of *this* compares with how many of *that*, you should know exactly why you want to know. How will you use that information? What business decisions will be made based on a movement of 5 to 10 percent in any one direction?

As an analyst you are inundated with requests for reports. You'll want to pay heed to Judah Phillips' advice in his post on the Web Analytics Demystified web site entitled "Thoughts on Prioritizing Web Analytics Work" (http://judah.webanalyticsdemystified.com/2008/10/thoughts-on-prioritizing-web-analytics-work.html), summarized here. How do you prioritize requests for analysis? Answer these questions:

♦ Is revenue at risk? (Always seems to be #1.)

♦ Who's asking? (As Bob Page from Yahoo! likes to say: All metrics are political.)

♦ How difficult is the request? (Do some, but not all, of the easy ones right away.)

♦ Can it be self-serviced? (Let them count cake!)

♦ When is the analysis needed? (Between immediately and 7.5 million years from now.)

♦ Why is the analysis needed? (This is the gotcha! question.)

Understanding Analysis

Are fat people lazy?

Pat LaPointe from MarketingNPV asked that question in an article for MediaPost (www.mediapost.com/publications/?fa=Articles.showArticle&art_aid=110610). He went on to explain how hard it is to provide a specific answer to a non-specific question. In order to answer this loaded question, one would have to:

1. Define "fat."

Weight/height ratios, body mass index, and body fat content are all legitimate options, but a common definition would have to be agreed to before calculations can begin.

2. Define "lazy."

Same problem. Levels of exercise? Work habits? Overreliance on modern conveniences?

3. Define the standard of proof.

Just how fat is fat and just how lazy is lazy?

4. Design a means of observing if the question is true.

Conduct the research and collect the data.

LaPointe then turned to "Is our marketing cost-effective?" and illustrated that these definitions are even more wobbly. He warned that the wobbility of these terms is exactly where politics enters the effort. Yes, Bob, all metrics are indeed political.

Therefore, you must first be certain that you know what you are trying to find out (what problem you are solving for) and then be certain that you and those around you agree on your definitions of the terms you use to describe and solve that problem.

It's also useful to understand how the mind works. In the introduction of his book *Psychology of Intelligence Analysis* (Center for the Study of Intelligence, Central Intelligence Agency, 1999), Richards J. Heuer, Jr. wrote:

> *People construct their own version of "reality" on the basis of information provided by the senses, but this sensory input is mediated by complex mental processes that determine which information is attended to, how it is organized, and the meaning attributed to it. What people perceive, how readily they perceive it, and how they process this information after receiving it are all strongly influenced by past experience, education, cultural values, role requirements, and organizational norms, as well as by the specifics of the information received.*

For some *very* useful and practical advice on approaching an analysis project, I can highly recommend *The Thinker's Guide to Analytical Thinking* by Dr. Linda Elder and Dr. Richard Paul (The Foundation for Critical Thinking, 2006) (www.criticalthinking.org).

Marketing Analysis and Optimization from 30,000 Feet

Divide each difficulty into as many parts as is feasible and necessary to resolve it.

— *René Descartes*

Knowing your goals, the company goals, and the limits of your budget for gathering and quantifying data are the entrance fee. If you don't feel as if you have a handle on your goals and resources, read on, but first place a rather large yellow sticky where you can't miss it, reminding you to find out fast.

If we consider the flow of the relationship between a company and a customer, we have a framework for addressing the metrics of each step in sequence. Optimizing your marketing is daunting, so you take it a step at a time.

Step one: Get their attention. You can't sell to somebody who has never heard of you. More on this in Chapter 2: Getting Attention—Reaching Your Audience.

Step two: Get them to like you. That's the subject of Chapter 4: Getting Emotional—Recognizing Sentiment.

Step three: Get them to interact. Chapter 5: Getting Response—Triggering Action

Step four: Convince them to buy. Chapter 5: Getting Response—Triggering Action

But none of that matters if you don't have goals. Start with an unremitting devotion to the things you want to see happen, divide each difficulty into as many parts as is feasible and necessary to resolve it, and you too can move up from stock clerk to history maker.

CHAPTER 2
Getting Attention—Reaching Your Audience

With clear goals in sight, the next step is getting your message to as many people as possible. This is a central factor of your eventual success. You cannot build a marketing sensation if the only ones who read your blog are your mother and your cat.

Awareness is the first step on the path to a long and profitable customer experience.

Awareness

Engagement

Persuasion

Conversion

Retention

We'll address measuring the response to your efforts (engagement) in Chapter 5. At this point, we'll focus on the number of people you reached with your posts, tweets, and uploads.

Can You Hear Me Now?

The classic definition of Reach is the percentage of people in the group you want to affect with your message. If you sell toothpaste, that's everybody with teeth. If you sell ice cream, that's everybody regardless of their dental situation. If you sell architects' supplies, your universe is much smaller.

Your means of reaching people used to be simple: newspaper, direct mail, television, radio, fliers on car windshields, doorknob hangers, trade shows, sandwich boards, and word-of-mouth. Social media is where word-of-mouth goes ballistic. Word-of-mouth doesn't happen by spontaneous generation, so the first thing you want to measure is the impact of that which you publish yourself.

"Reach" refers to the percent of the population you want to touch that you can actually get a hold of. If you sell supplies and services to architects in Chicago and three quarters of them read one trade journal, an ad in that magazine gives you a reach of 75 percent. It doesn't mean they have necessarily seen your ad; it means you have created an opportunity for them to see it.

Put up a billboard on the highway and so many thousand commuters have an "opportunity to see" your message. Unless they were texting, applying makeup, tuning the radio, disciplining their kids, or heaven forbid, watching traffic. Put an ad on TV and so many million viewers have an "opportunity to see" your message. Unless they were fast-forwarding, texting, applying makeup, tuning the radio, disciplining their kids, or, most likely, answering nature's call. Or the phone.

Send out a message online and some unknown number of people will have the opportunity to see it—if they have already subscribed, befriended, or followed you or know somebody who did. And the glory of social networking is that they might only have known somebody who knew somebody who knew somebody . . . who did.

Frequency is simply the number of times you have produced an "opportunity to see" in a given time period. Sometimes it only takes one glance for somebody to know they want and need you to create their Semi-Submersible Offshore Drilling Rig Scale Model (Figure 2.1).

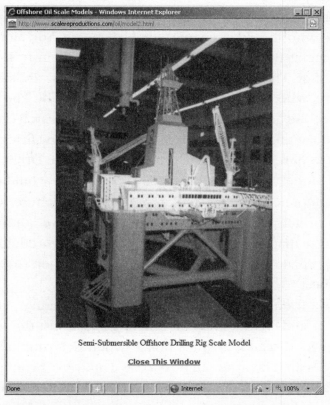

Figure 2.1 Scale Reproductions, LLC counts on their photo gallery to incite prospective customers to Contact Us.

Scale Reproductions, LLC

Figure 2.2   This decidedly uninspiring yet clearly communicative logo may require 100 viewings before it is memorable.

In other cases, they may have to have seen your logo 50 times before it occurs to them to call you in their hour of need (Figure 2.2).

Prospective customers are a mix of those who should be interested in your products and those who already are. Those who should, are your target of choice. You aim your message at them and try your best to get them to look at your offer. Those who *are* interested right now are looking for you, whether you think they should be or not. You hope this second group is going to find you—via a search engine.

You might have had no expectation that a law firm might want to purchase a Semi-Submersible Offshore Drilling Rig Scale Model, so you didn't market to them. It would make no economic sense to send a direct mail brochure to law firms or activate a telemarketing plan. If there is just one out there that is thinking about how your models could help them explain something to a judge and jury, then Google is your best friend.

Best friends need love and attention. Blogging, writing articles, and commenting on others' blogs is just the sort of spider food search engines utilize when determining relevancy. Search ranking can be used as a metric for your social media progress, but only as a proxy. Reach is a fuzzy number to start with and this takes it a step further out of focus.

If you really want to know if the world has heard of you, you have to go ask them. One at a time.

1. Have you ever heard of Scale Reproductions, Inc.?

2. Did you know Scale Reproductions' first scale model was a plank-style shrimp boat commissioned by its owner in Bayou La Batre, Alabama?

3. Did you know that Scale Reproductions sells to companies such as General Dynamics, Northrop Grumman, Newport News Shipbuilding, and Raytheon?

Asking these questions over time and across geographies lets you build up a trend map of brand awareness. But just because they've heard of you does not necessarily mean they know what you stand for. They may not know that's how you like to be characterized. That takes more questions and is referred to as brand recognition.

Brand Recognition

In the dance that is advertising, marketing, and sales, the first step is being seen. You can stand on a street corner and hand out fliers. You can paste a huge sign on the side of a building. You can mail a postcard to a million people. You can broadcast your message to multiple millions. The glory of social media is that you can get your would-be customers to spread the message for you—if you're really good and really lucky.

The result of being good and lucky is that people remember your company name, your logo, the products you sell and the characteristics that you'd like them to associate with the company.

Chances are excellent that you recognize this fragment of this logo (Figure 2.3). Their brand is so well-known and so familiar that this is more than enough for brand recognition.

Figure 2.3 Just a fragment of this logo is probably enough for you to name the man and the company.

They have achieved what Martin Lindstrom likes to call Smashing Your Brand (www.martinlindstrom.com/index.php/cmsid_list_articles/_49).

Back in 1915 Earl R. Dean, who was working at the Root Glass Company, was given a brief to design a bottle, which firstly could be recognized in the dark. And then, even if broken, a person could tell at first glance what it was.

The result was the Coca-Cola bottle—a shape so distinctive that you could see a broken piece of it on the ground and recognize the product.

From the logo fragment in Figure 2.3, you could likely name the company, the product, the founder, and their slogan. You could correctly associate a handful of characteristics to the brand.

Kentucky Fried Chicken

Finger Lickin' Good

Colonel Sanders

Secret Recipe

11 Secret Herbs & Spices

Fast Food

Inexpensive

KFC's logo was so well-known that when it came time to announce a new version, they decided to create an example that could be seen from space (Figure 2.4).

This 87,500 square foot logo was placed in the Nevada desert in November 2006 to attract media attention. They set up 65,000 square tiles as "pixels" and included a coupon code for those willing to zoom in and hunt for it.

Figure 2.4   There's no mistaking the Colonel—even from outer space.

You know your brand is successful if it is top-of-mind when the public is asked about a given category. You say toothpaste; they say Crest. You say airline; they say United. You say cola; they say Coke. This is brand recall. Getting your brand recognized is part of Awareness. It's getting the attributes associated with your brand that constitutes true recognition.

Brand Attribute Recognition

What attributes does the company want the public to associate with their brand?

Nike = self-confidence and power

7-11 = convenience

Wal-Mart = low prices

Apple = style

Kodak = family moments

Coke = refreshing

You may or may not agree with my impression of these brands—and therein lies the problem. You'll need to listen hard to the buzz of social media to capture whether the characteristics you want to be associated with your brand really are.

We'll take a deeper look at the art of online listening in Chapter 6: Getting the Message—Hearing the Conversation.

So now you know if they've heard of you and if they remember your stated unique sales proposition. Do they like what you stand for? We'll dip into brand affinity in Chapter 4: Getting Emotional—Recognizing Sentiment and brand engagement in Chapter 5: Getting Response—Triggering Action.

Business Blogging Metrics

For now, let's stick with measuring your ability to get your message out there in the first place: your own blog.

You can publish your message via a press release, direct mail drop, radio ad, TV spot, etc. You can also publish online via:

Article

E-mail

Blog post

Podcast

Photo

Video

Twitter

Or some means invented after this book hit the streets

Measuring the reach and recognition of a message distributed online is the same across the variety of channels, with a few twists along the way.

If you're blogging for the sake of making a name for yourself, you can create your own stable of metrics for calculating the psychic, emotional, and ego value of blogging. ("Hey. Mom, look at meeee!") Watching the growing number of people who subscribe and follow you is fun and heartwarming, but that's not instructive when it comes to deciding how much to invest in corporate blogging.

If you're a publisher, you measure the number of people who show up and the number of additional clicks you can get out of them. You want to show advertisers that they should place their ads on your properties. In April

2006, Jason Stamper took a calculated stab at "The ROI of blogging" and came up with the following formula (www.businessreviewonline.com/blog/archives/2006/04/the_roi_of_blog.html):

> *(F)or sites with advertising, that don't tend to generate many useful leads for the marketing department, I came up with BVIa—for Blog Value Index a. It's a simple equation to work out in quantitative terms whether the blog is paying for itself or costing the company money.*
>
> *If you pump your figures into the equation and the BVI comes out at less than one, then the blog is costing the company money, and if the index comes out greater than one, it's generating profit. In all these equations I assume the cost of blog software and hosting and the like is zero—it's not expensive and usually covered under a company's other hosting costs anyway.*
>
> *Here's the equation:*

$$BVIa = \frac{adh\ (aay/1,000)}{abt \times ehw}$$

Jason's equation uses the following variables:

adh = average daily hits

aay = average advertising yield

abt = average number of hours spent per day blogging

ehw = the employee hourly wage of the blogger

I take immediate exception to the use of the word "hits." I dismissed that term in my book on online advertising published in 1997 by quoting Katherine Paine, CEO of The Delahaye Group, as standing for "How Idiots Track Success." I'm sure Jason wasn't referring to the technically accurate definition of how many individual files the server served where a single page can be made up of dozens of files. However, it's not clear if he meant page views or people.

As there are far more companies who are selling goods and services than there are publishers selling advertising, I'm much more interested in the business value of a blog to those companies.

The first formal social media expert was Forrester Research analyst Charlene Li. She got a lot of attention for a blog entry in October 2006 called Calculating the ROI of blogging. It included the following chart.

Benefit	Appropriate Measurement
Consumer self-education	Higher conversion rate for blog visitors
Greater visibility in search results	Increased traffic from search to blog
Lower the cost of public relations	Generate the same level of awareness as PR
Reach an enthusiast community	Lower cost communication tool
Address criticisms on other blogs/news stories	Measure the slow down of bad news spreading
More responsive to consumer concerns	Track customer satisfaction and retention
Improve employee innovation and productivity	Track employee satisfaction and retention
Improved stock price with greater visibility into the organization	Connect improved investor sentiment to blog readership

http://blogs.forrester.com/groundswell/2006/10/calculating_the.html

Conceptually, Charlene was right on the money, but she stopped short of actually counting the money. For that, we turn to her book. This is the "ROI of an executive's blog" table from *Groundswell: Winning in a World Transformed by Social Technologies*, which Charlene Li co-authored with Josh Bernoff (Forrest Research, Inc., 2008).

Start-Up Costs	
Planning and development	$25K
Training for blogging executive	10K
Ongoing costs (annual)	
Blogging platform	25K
Brand-monitoring service	50K
IT support	3K
Content production, including executive time	150K
Review and redirection	20K
Total costs, year one	**$283K**
Benefit analysis (annual)	
Advertising value: visibility/traffic (estimate 7,500 daily page views at a $2.50 cost per thousand)	$7K
PR value; press stories about/driven from blog content (estimate 24 stories at value of $10K each)	240K
Word-of-mouth value: referring posts on other medium- to high-profile blogs (estimate 370 posts at value of $100 each)	37K
Support value: support calls avoided because of information on blog (estimate 50 daily support calls avoided at $5.50 per call)	69K
Research value: customer insights (estimate comments/feedback equivalent to 5 focus groups at $8K each)	50K
Total benefits, year one	**$393K**

In his latest book, *Web Analytics 2.0: The Art of Online Accountability and Science of Customer Centricity* (Sybex,

October 26, 2009), web analytics evangelist and top blogger Avinash Kaushik adds Opportunity Cost to the mix.

> *If you did not blog, the resources you put into blogging would go elsewhere, into a project that could earn you money. That is opportunity cost. You may have a great patentable idea or a solution to the Middle East crisis—these ideas are worth a lot. You need to price out your ideas.*
>
> *If I apply this concept to myself, I know that if I were not blogging, I could be paid for other work. I could perhaps work a part-time job analyzing reports for a company and get paid $100,000 a year.*
>
> *Opportunity cost = $100,000.*
>
> *So, either way, if you use time as a measure or the earning power of that time, you can come up with a cost of blogging. It is important to compute this cost for your company or for your personal efforts.*

Advertising, PR, word-of-mouth, support cost savings, and opportunity costs . . . Let's start simple and look at the basics of "reach." How many saw what you wrote and how many got the message?

How Many Saw What You Wrote?

While this is the simplest question, it is not simple to answer.

The easiest number to acquire is how many people came to your blog page. That's either in your web analytics tool if your blog is on your own site or a number that your blog hosting service provides.

If all goes well, a growing number of people will subscribe to your blog via RSS feed and view it through a feed reader. FeedBurner and other tools will help track how many subscribers you have, but unlike e-mail subscribers, this is not a fixed, known number but one that is derived. People do not enter their name and address into your database but tune in to your broadcast signal. Here's how FeedBurner describes it at www.google.com/support/feedburner:

> *FeedBurner's subscriber count is based on an approximation of how many times your feed has been requested in a 24-hour period. Subscribers is inferred from an analysis of the many different feed readers and aggregators that retrieve this feed daily. Subscribers is not computed for browsers and bots that access your feed.*
>
> *Subscribers counts are calculated by matching IP address and feed reader combinations, then using our detailed understanding of the multitude of readers, aggregators, and bots on the market to make additional inferences.*

So if I fired up my reader today and had subscribed to your feed at some point in the past, your readership would be incremented by one. But just like e-mail, the fact that I subscribed and was fed your message does not necessarily mean I read your every word. It's up to individual subscribers to actually read and internalize what you were trying to communicate.

Google's FeedBurner also reports on "reach," which is "the total number of people who have taken action—viewed or clicked—on the content in your feed."

Subscribers is a measure of how many people are subscribed to your feed. At any given time, you can expect that a certain percentage of this subscriber base is actively engaging with your content and this "Reach" measurement provides this additional insight.

Additionally, there may be people viewing your content beyond your known subscriber base. For example, they may view your content on a feed search engine or news filter site.

Reach aggregates both of these groups, providing an accurate and useful measurement of your true audience.

Now we have an approximation of your readership, and like all numbers on the Internet, this one has no value by itself. It's only when you compare that number with your own baseline or compare it with your competition that you have the necessary context to determine how well you're doing. That context is essential if you intend to use these measurements to make business decisions.

How Many Got the Message?

Avinash Kaushik had a one-month head start on Charlene Li in 2006 with the first of a series of posts that were more operational and tactical in nature. While many blogging platforms will report on how many times your various posts were viewed, Avinash took a crack at measuring the number of people who read his blog and explained himself in a post called How to Measure Success of a Blog (120 Days in Numbers) (www.kaushik.net/avinash/2006/09/how-to-measure-success-of-a-blog.html).

*My proposal is to compute a metric called Blog
Readership (and its "web analytics" equivalent
Blog Unique Readership). It is derived from two
different sources, the web analytics tool and the
RSS tool (and one leap of faith).*

	Month 1	Month 2	Month 3	Month 4	"Total"
Total Visitors	*4,735*	*8,784*	*5,767*	*6,525*	*25,811*
Unique Visitors	*2,000*	*4,230*	*2,515*	*3,162*	*10,791*
Avg Daily Feed Subscribers	*50*	*117*	*241*	*360*	*–*
Feed Subscribers	*1,554*	*3,626*	*7,471*	*11,151*	*23,802*
Feed "Unique" Subscribers	*200*	*468*	*964*	*1,440*	*–*
"Blog Readership"	*6,289*	*12,410*	*13,238*	*17,676*	*49,613*
"Blog Unique Readership"	*2,200*	*4,698*	*3,479*	*4,602*	*–*

1. *Get* **Total Visitors** *(or Visits or Visitors) from
   your Web Analytics tool.*

2. *Get the* **Average Daily Feed Subscribers** *for
   each month. (I use FeedBurner for RSS stats).*

3. *Get your* **Monthly Feed "Subscribers"**
   *number (sum of each day's subscribers from
   FeedBurner).*

4. *To get a best estimate of your* **Feed's
   "Unique" Subscribers** *multiply your feed
   subscriber number by 4. (Sort of inspired by
   Greg Linden's reference* [http://glinden.blog

spot.com/2006/09/1000th-post-on-geeking-with-greg.html]. *Update: Please see Greg's comment below* [http://www.kaushik.net/avinash/2006/09/how-to-measure-success-of-a-blog.html#comment-3664] *and also my reply* [http://www.kaushik.net/avinash/2006/09/how-to-measure-success-of-a-blog.html#comment-3684] *for more context.)*

5. *Now your* **Monthly Blog Readership** = *Total Visitors* + *Feed "Visitors"*

6. *And your, again best estimate,* **Monthly Blog Unique Readership** = *Unique Visitors* + *Feed "Unique" Subscribers.*

As you can see, even a question as simple as "How many people?" can be tricky at best.

Avinash has updated his calculation of readership a couple of times on his Occam's Razor blog, and I recommend a trip to www.kaushik.net to see what he's written lately.

Web sites like PostRank (Figure 2.5) are lending a hand in getting your arms around how popular your blog might be.

A Little Bird Told Me: Twitter Numbers

Measuring Twitter is almost the same as measuring your blog. Almost.

Again, if your goal is personal aggrandizement, you can track that with tools like Buzzcom (www.buzzcom.com) (Figure 2.6). If that's your reason for blogging and tweeting, just try to avoid showing up too often on http://tweetingtoohard.com.

Figure 2.5 PostRank helps keep tabs on brand mentions.

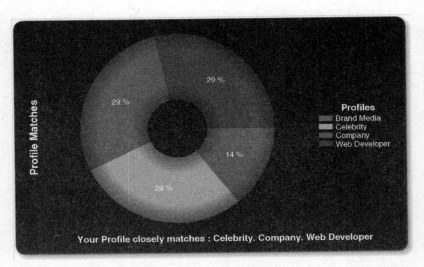

Figure 2.6 Your profile may closely match a corporate celebrity web developer, but the business implications are "not clear at this time."

The number of followers you have may be indicative of popularity but not of consumption. People's following behaviors run the gamut from those who read every tweeter they follow (me) and those who follow everybody and anybody. It's like your ratio of e-mail subscribers to readers. You don't really know if they're reading your tweets.

Fortunately, you *can* measure if they passed your words along. Retweeting is a solid measure of public opinion about the value of your tweets. Chances are excellent that a tweet about your lunch plans is not likely to be passed along (Figure 2.7).

When you *do* have something to say that strikes a chord with your target audience, they will trip over themselves to be the first one to repeat it. Here's where the electronic, social word-of-mouth kicks your reach into high gear. Each retweeter is standing on your shoulders to improve your reach.

Figure 2.7 Friends don't let friends tweet banalities for business.

Lots of tools are out there to help you monitor what pearls of your wisdom others deem worthy of retweeting. Between Tweetbeep, trackbacks, and Google Alerts, you'll be able to maintain your vigilant brand-spread watch.

By tracking your retweets, you can add up:

♦ How many followers you have.

♦ How many of them retweeted.

♦ How many followers they have.

♦ How many of those followers retweeted.

♦ And so on.

This allows you to estimate how many people had the opportunity to see your message (Figure 2.8).

The same concept can be used for measuring the reach of a blog post. If others comment about your post and trackback to it, you can scratch out a back-of-the-envelope estimate of the impact of that shout heard 'round the world.

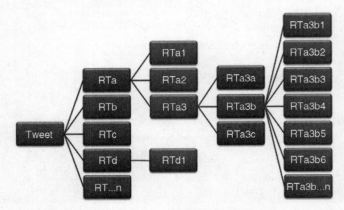

Figure 2.8 Tweeting can cause a cascade of retweets.

Turing Test

The usual caution for measuring anything online is in play here: Be certain you can tell whether you are measuring human activity or bot activity.

This is not to say that robots are bad—it's just important to know the difference. Robots can scrape, follow, friend, tweet, and retweet, and while that sounds like an abomination of the intent of a social network, bear in mind that one of those nodes in Figure 2.8 may indeed be a small piece of software somewhere.

When it's time to tote up how many "people" had an opportunity to see your message, make sure you're only counting the people. When you think about influence (see Chapter 3: Getting Respect—Identifying Influence), then the complexity becomes even more multifaceted.

The really tricky bit about tracking retweets is that they tend to morph from one to the next, just like that good old game of Telephone. People change the tweets they repeat so a strict algorithm of looking for the same phrase is going to run into trouble. The paper "Tweet, Tweet, Retweet: Conversational Aspects of Retweeting on Twitter" (www.danah.org/papers/TweetTweetRetweet.pdf), published in the IEEE Proceedings of HICCS-43 (January 2010), describes how human nature confounds Twitter tracking tools. The paper states, "Given the inherent difficulty in keeping track of who truly pays attention to whom is hopeless."

Twitter Case Study

Adam Greco is director of Web Analytics at Salesforce.com, which makes him responsible for measuring everything online right up until people log into salesforce.com as a customer. Salesforce.com is now in the listening stage—monitoring how often they are talked about in various channels.

"We're trying to find out who's talking about us, who's talking about our competitors and figure out what they're saying. We're doing out bound as well—we have a whole YouTube channel and a Facebook channel with one or two people who just focus on getting our message out, but I'm analyzing what people are saying about us."

Adam integrated Omniture's SiteCatalyst with Twitter, creating a list of three types of keywords. First is their branded keywords that mention their company. The second group is competitor keywords. The third group is general, industry keywords they care about. "So for example in our case, 'cloud computing' or 'CRM.' Using the Twitter API, we go out to Twitter and pull any tweets that mention those phrases on an hourly basis. So, we now have charts and graphs to monitor over time and we can be alerted through the e-mail or a cell phone device if there's a spike."

Managing by alarm is a time-honored tradition. There is a certain background noise level to be calibrated. A certain number of mentions is normal traffic. Should the general tweeting public stop talking about the company altogether, then the PR and marketing departments need to be notified that their latest efforts are not keeping the brand in the minds, hearts, and voices of the marketplace. Should the noise level jump, PR, marketing, and customer service need to investigate and quell the fears or fan the excitement.

Salesforce.com is interested in more than just the audio volume of the discussion. They want to know how large an audience a given discussion is reaching. "The second thing we do is pull in a tweet ID through the API along with all of the metadata associated with that tweet; the actual tweet itself, the 140 characters, the author, who the tweet was directed to if anyone. How many followers does that person have? How many friends does that person have?

"We're also looking at grabbing the name of the Twitter client. If someone comes to my site from twitter.com, I can see all the (Omniture) 'success events' that take place because they have a referring domain and I can say, 'Oh, I had a thousand people from twitter.com fill out forms.' But if they come from TweetDeck or Twirl, I have no referrer data. I can't count those toward social media. They look like they typed in the URL directly. It would be great if those Twitter client companies would pass referrer information so we can give them credit for the success that they are generating. Once I have that, I can get a better handle on how much of my overall traffic is Twitter related and helps me allocate promotional expenditures."

Adam is tracking social media mentioned over time and following the trends and can calculate mine share.

(Continued)

(*Continued*)

How visible are their competitors? Are there any new companies coming into the marketplace? Any new technologies? Any old competitors doing something new?

The next step is looking for what Adam calls little nuggets of gold. "I am keenly interested in the tweets where we are mentioned along with our competitors, which gives me not just competitive information but comparative information. I can keep an eye on how we are generally compared by the public.

"Any mention of our CEO's name gets automatically routed to the PR department to monitor reputational risk. Any mention of a particular feature or product gets routed to the appropriate product manager.

"One of the most important parts of this is that tweets actually disappear after some period of time. Twitter does not infinitely store tweets or at least they don't make them findable yet. So now you have all the tweets that are relevant to you in Omniture, stored for eternity. Now, you could actually go back the last two years and say, 'Show me all tweets that say this word over the last two years.'"

That said, the deep analysis of comment trending over time is yet to come. Adam has only been collecting comments for a few months. "So far, I've spent most of my time just figuring on how we collect everything. My vision is taking the metrics that we have like salesforce.com visits, unique visitors, form completes, and form completion rate and juxtapose that with what's happening out on social media and look for correlations. I want to see if we have a spike in Twitter, do we get a corresponding spike in form fill-outs, and how many of those end up actually becoming customers? And so, can I make a causal relationship between a social media and new leads or closed business?"

Adam plans on tracking back to the original tweeter. "We should be able to connect the dots. Every time this person tweets, we get a 2 percent lift in form completions. So let's make sure that we keep this person really happy. I'd love to merge that with (Omniture's) Test and Target (multivariate testing tool). Then, if we see a huge spike in tweets about customer service in salesforce.com, the stuff on our homepage could be reflective of what's going out on Twitter."

"We're watching search as well," says Adam. "Here's how many visits we got from this term through natural search, paid search, and from this same term in a Tweet, and we can now add those together and see what our total brand value is of salesforce.com across search and social media. Anytime someone comes from a social media site like LinkedIn, Twitter, or Facebook, we track that as a special referral called social media so that we can show that alongside the paid search."

The future holds a lot in store for salesforce.com if Adam gets his way. He sees a day when they can track from the outbound tweet to the quality of visitor coming back. Then they will know if the traffic generated by the tweet, blogpost, or other comment out there in Social Media Land is quality traffic; traffic with higher conversion rates, turning social media acquaintances into profitable customers.

Figure 2.9   Anybody with a bone to pick can create a tarnish-intending web site.

Measure the Reach of What Is Published About You

There are those who repeated what you had to say and there are those who have their own thoughts about your brand, your company, and your products to share.

Much of what makes the rounds in these regards are the I or We Hate You sites (Figure 2.9).

We'll save those for Chapter 6: Getting the Message—Hearing the Conversation as well. For now, we want to identify those sites and blogs that mention your company or product in a neutral or positive way so we can tally your reach.

Simple tools like Google Alerts can keep you apprised of mentions of specific keywords in the blogs, as can Technorati. More sophisticated services like Hitwise and comScore can do so much more, but will also deliver the goods on how many people are talking about you out there.

But don't stop at Twitter and Blogs. Keep your eyes and ears open to photos posted about you on Flickr, Twitpic, Yfrog, videos on YouTube and many, many others. Fortunately, there are a myriad of services like Buzzlogic and Blogscope to help you do just that.

There are also a number of walled gardens that deserve your attention—the social networking sites.

Measuring Social Networking Sites

At first, only those named Dilbert could create their own web sites. Then, a few years before blogging hit the scene, social networking was all the rage. MySpace, Facebook, and LinkedIn not only offered a place to represent yourself, but to connect with your friends and colleagues. Companies are trying to use these networks to connect with their customers. Some are doing it well and some are not. How about you? What should you measure?

Just what we've covered above, but in a smaller arena. The blogosphere and Twitter are open while the social networks are closed. You must be a member. Therefore, you'll need different tools and techniques for keeping an eye on whether people are becoming a fan of your product page, talking about you, sharing the opinions of others with each other, etc.

Measure Your Audience

Kyle Flaherty is currently Director of Marketing and Social Media at BreakingPoint Systems and told this story on Jennifer Leggio's Social Business Blog at ZDNet (http://blogs.zdnet.com/feeds/?p=321&page=2).

Kyle explained that social media was one of the top traffic referrers for technology startup BreakingPoint as they promoted a webinar. He considered costs like personnel time and tool fees and balanced them against sales that could be attributed to the webinar.

At the time he posted his experience, it took a lot of different tools to bring the data together: Blip.tv, BUDurl, Eloqua, GetClicky, Google Analytics, Google Reader, HubSpot, and others.

Said Kyle, "Using BUDurl I can tell how many folks have signed up for the webinar through Twitter, I use GetClicky to see the folks who went to the webinar page from our LinkedIn Group, and I'll even be able to view the folks who watch the webinar live on USTREAM the day of the event. We can see how many participants then sign up for a product demo, choose to do a product evaluation, and ultimately buy the product.

The trick is always to fit the direct link between promotional activities and revenue in order to show value and make a case for a bonus. Once you've made that link, says Kyle, you can "continue your work with the community, which coincidentally lets you dismantle the importance of ROI internally and start to focus on IOR . . . Impact of Relationships."

The Internet is full of places where people can congregate. It is your responsibility to monitor them and keep tabs on the conversation. That changes slightly when it's not exactly a conversation you are tracking. Got widgets?

Measure Your Apps and Widgets

A simple application on Facebook can have a great impact or can fall flat. It can achieve great virality and impact sales or it can achieve great virality and have no impact on sales whatsoever.

In 2007, Johnson & Johnson created a Facebook application called the "Acuvue Wink." Like poking somebody or sending them a drink, this app let you choose the animated pair of winking eyes and the message to send to your friends. This time, the branding worked. When the campaign was at its peak, 10,000 Facebook users were "winking" every day. Some 65,000 people downloaded the app between the beginning of August and the end of the year. They were hoping to reach 100,000 people and got a half million individuals. On the frequency scale, they were shooting for a half million winks and went over a million, or two winks per person. But above all, sales of the 1-Day Acuvue Moist contact lenses went up by 17 percent.

Yes, you can budget for creating a campaign that you want to go viral. Yes, you can plan it. But you can't count on it. If it happens, the numbers will let you know that you've got a breakthrough promotion on your hands. The Wink application was something easy for Facebook users to use, but the reach of that program was only activated when somebody thought to wink somebody else. A widget has a different lifecycle and a few more metrics.

Rather than click a button and use your application, Facebookers can place your widget on their page so that all their friends can see it when they show up. The widget adopter does not have to set it in motion; it simply waits until one of those friends sees it, uses it, and maybe puts it on their own page.

When I need details about widgets, I turn to Jodi McDermott, director of Data Strategy and Analytics at Clearspring (www.Clearspring.com). Jodi is very active on the Web Analytics Association Standards Committee, and in July 2009, the WAA created a draft set of Social Media Standards. These definitions help us communicate clearly but also provide an understanding of the sorts of things that can be measured.

For example, you can measure the number of times a widget is Grabbed by a member of the public. A consumer Grabs the widget from the creator in order to Install it, and each Installation is an independently running instance of the software. The widget might have to be used for the first time to confirm an installation. When the widget is activated by a visitor to the widget host's page, the widget software loads, and that constitutes a View. A quick glance at what can be measured helps explain the Life of a Widget (Table 2.1).

Table 2.1   The Life of a Widget

Hosted	The author puts it somewhere—or many somewheres—so the public can be exposed to it.
Viewed	Someone looks at the page where the widget is hosted. Similar to an ad impression.
Grabbed	A viewer takes the widget from the hosted page to use on their web site.
Install	A viewer becomes a new host.
Active	A widget that is viewed within a set time frame. A widget may get installed but never viewed.
Uninstall	The new host removes the widget.
Mouseover	A viewer moves the mouse cursor over the widget to interact with it.
Time on page	The widget can update the author that it is still on a page being viewed.
Event	Internal interactivity—clicking on tabs, playing videos, etc.

Your widget may be hugely popular by people who want to grab it and install it, but if it's never viewed your success isn't complete. It's great that thousands of people had a high enough affinity with your brand to want your widget, but that only creates an opportunity to see. But an unviewed widget is as useless as a billboard in the dark.

Jodi was careful to set the proper level of expectation when it comes to the expectation that all of the measurements are precise. She outlined a number of problems that can crop up using widgets that I had left out of my Media-Post article on fuzzy numbers. See "The Numbers Just Don't Add Up" below.

The Numbers Just Don't Add Up

(Originally published on Mediapost.com)

A funny thing happened on the way to the CMO's office.

Between the realization of an eye-opening, game-changing insight gleaned from advertising test results and web behavior data, the report you were gleefully ferrying to the C-Suite wilted, turned brown at the edges and started to dribble a slimy substance with a conspicuous stench.

The CMO immediately developed a nose-squint. The VP of Corporate Communications had that "Oooo, you're in for it!" look in her eye and the VP of Advertising nudged the Director of Direct Marketing and said sotto-voce, "The golden boy is about to find out his day in the sun has turned him to toast."

The CMO pointed to (but did not touch):

A traffic report from comScore

A traffic report from Hitwise

A chart from Compete.com

An ad banner report from Atlas

A traffic report from Omniture

Another from Google Analytics

"It's like the old joke," she says with no humor at all. "If you take all the economists in the world and line them up end-to-end, they all point different directions. What the hell is going on with these numbers? Are we getting 32.5 million people on our web site or 44 million?"

The first time you ran into this nest of nettles, you hopped over to the white board and cheerfully explained all about:

Cookie deletion

Cookie blocking

Multiple machine browsing

Multiple browser browsing

Multiple people on the same cookie

Non-human traffic

Dynamic IP addressing

Page caching

Javascript loading

Called pixel placement

You didn't even get to the good stuff about comparing miles to gallons and how:

Different tools using

Different date cut-off routines and

Different methods to capture

Different types of data to store in

Different kinds of databases with a

Different method of data cleansing and

Different slicing and dicing segmentation to produce

Different kinds of reports that ended up in

Different feed for integration into

Different datawarehouses

. . . before you were thanked for your help and shown the door—permanently.

You don't fall for it this time.

This time you explain that the world of online marketing has been suffering from a delusion of precision and an expectation of exactitude.

You tell them that we live in a world of statistics and probabilities. We can't count all the stars in the sky so we don't try. We don't try to get an actual count of:

Television watchers

Radio listeners

Magazine readers

Billboard readers

Bus poster readers

Floor sticker readers

Airline ticket jacket readers

Sandwich board readers

Instead, we count some and estimate the rest.

You share the good news that we can do this better than any of the above—and we've got some astonishing tools and techniques for dynamically targeting the audience and optimizing each one's experience.

You say, "We get 36.3 million people coming to our web site."

She lowers her half-glasses and gives you the look you last saw when caught using the office copy machine for party invitations. So you add, "With a 4% margin of error and it's a benchmark we can compare month over month from now on."

"So somewhere between 34.5 and 38 million."

"Pretty much right between them, in fact."

Disparagingly she asks, "You really can't give me a more accurate number of how many people saw this digital marketing masterpiece that costs me tens of millions a year?"

"I can tell you whether our digital visitors are more engaged with our brand, come back more often, buy from us and discuss our products with their friends. How many people buy our products who saw our ads on CNN and *Oprah* that cost you *hundreds* of millions a year?"

The VP of Advertising makes himself visibly smaller.

"I came here to show you a way that could save four million dollars of search marketing while boosting online sales by six to eight percent."

The scowl leaves the CMO's face. The odor of dubious data dissipates, the conversation suddenly immaterial. Her eyes narrow as she leans forward and says, "Show me."

The numbers don't have to be precise—just compelling.

To this list, Jodi added the vagaries of measuring active content across disparate properties that are managed by human beings.

"It's not easy," she agreed. "You run into the same issues that you have with standard web analytics; the domain doesn't always come through like you would expect it, the data doesn't always parse. There are, what I call environmental challenges where the API from the social network that's feeding data back to a service provider is changed without notice. We're in such early days that we don't always have world class teams in engineering and operations on every one of these social networking platforms."

This market is rife with start-ups in college dorms, and functional genius and technical prowess do not necessarily come with engineering or business process rigor. They seldom have enterprise-level data centers providing solid, reliable platforms.

"And," smiles Jodi, "they're scrappy. They like changing things on the fly daily for fun. On your own web site, you can go down and work with IT and make sure things are tagged and standardized and notified. Here, there's such an incredible interdependency.

"But," she reassures me, "with more large movie studios using widgets and the telecoms counting on widgets to help stay competitive, the infrastructure is getting much better. The technical side is discovering what works, and there are some generally accepted coding practices that developers know they have to live up to. It's early days but not for long.

Where there's big money being spent, the technology finds a way to live up to expectations."

Has Your Message Been Heard?

Reach is all about how many people had the opportunity to see your brand in general and your message in particular. It's all about the possibility that the outbound message might be heard above the pandemonium of the modern marketing environment:

> Whether your message is consumed is a matter of guesswork

> Whether your message is retained is a matter of market research and surveys.

> Whether your message is reaching just the right people to propel it out to others . . . is an excellent question.

CHAPTER 3

Getting Respect—Identifying Influence

Social media is the connective tissue of social networks. Social networks make it clear that what you know is important, but who you know is critical.

If you tell Fred and he tells Sally and John, that's great.

But if Sally and John tell Robert and Guy and Seth, then things really start to happen. What makes Robert, Guy, and Seth more valuable when it comes to message transmission than John, Sally, or Fred? Three things:

1. The size of their audience.

2. Their degree of connectedness.

3. The power of their voice.

Let's start with the easy stuff: What is their first-level reach?

How Big Is Their Audience?

If Henry finds something interesting enough to tweet, then we can count his Twitter followers as a starting point. If he posts it on his blog, we can count his subscribers. These represent his first-level reach.

But the numbers suddenly get more interesting when we parse out the types of followers and subscribers we might be counting. Each type of devotees has a different value. Let's assign a score to each type starting with Subscribers and Followers.

Type of Node	Value
Subscribers and Followers	1
Readers	1
Fans	2
Repeaters	4

SUBSCRIBERS AND FOLLOWERS

At one point in time, subscribers and followers expressed enough interest to click that button that says "I want to know more." But that was once upon a time. Are they living happily ever after or, like the recipient of a gift subscription to a magazine from a doting aunt, do they simply ignore each issue, tweet, or post? Until we know more, we're only awarding these people one point.

Lots of people subscribe, great. But do they read?

READERS

Readers come in two flavors—those who subscribe and read and those who read without subscribing. If I see a tweet from Mike who retweeted something from Ryland and click through to the blog post, press release, article, etc., then I am a casual, one-time reader. I'm worth one point. Ryland is a subscriber and reader so he's worth two points.

FANS

Fans have expressed their delight with a different kind of click. Not only are they subscribers, they want others to know about their affiliation with the brand or person. These people are worth two points. If Ryland happens to be a fan as well as a subscriber and a reader, his value to the organization is now four.

Thomas Baekdal of the eponymous Baekdal.com online magazine decided to take the measure of a fan and wrote about it in August 2009.

> *And the short story is that one active fan is worth 445 people. And you need to reach 14,000 people to get one active fan. Which also means that only 56 active fans can create just as much exposure than [sic] a web site with 25,000 visitors.*

Thomas started by defining a fan as "one who either follows everything you do, or actively points other people to you—or both." He segments them into three types:

1. Fans, subscribers, or followers on your social channels (like Twitter, Facebook, FriendFeed, etc.).

2. RSS subscribers.

3. People who keep coming back to your site (at least once every week).

Thomas accounted for absolute unique visitors to his web site, new fans on social channels (Twitter, Facebook, etc.), RSS subscribers, repeat visitors, people sharing content (mentions), and second layer followers/fans.

From that, he calculated that he needed to reach 407,406 visitors to get 3,854 new fans across all channels, or 106 visitors yielded one fan. Looking at banner ads, he determined (with an average click-through rate in general at 0.2 percent) he needed 53,000 impressions to get 106 visitors to produce one fan.

Realizing that only 179 out of 24,108 fans were active (retweet or share content), Thomas determined that he'd need 7,049,000 ad impressions to get one active fan. His active fans have an average of 445 fans, so when 15 people comment on an image uploaded to Facebook, they multiply the message to 6,675 others, making them much more valuable.

At the end of all his machinations, Thomas concluded that one active fan is worth 445 regular visitors and will generate four new fans every month. It takes more than 14,000 visitors to generate a single active fan, but it only takes 106 visitors to create a passive fan.

REPEATERS

You know your message is valuable when it is repeated. Let's call that "honorable mentions." Granted, they might mention you in ways less than affirmative but let's hold off on that conversation for Chapter 4: Getting Emotional—Recognizing the Sentiment.

When a tree falls in a forest and there is nobody there to hear it, it makes no difference whether it makes a sound or not. If a leaf falls in a forest and there are thousands standing within earshot, the sound is so minute, it makes no difference.

Mike is a repeater. He saw something interesting from Ryland and passed it along. The score for a repeater might be a calculation based on how many people subscribe, read, and repeat, but Mike might not be a subscriber or a repeater. We very quickly get into complex numbers.

You might also want to weight these scores for tweets vs. blogs, as a tweet is time-dependent. Not only do people tend to ignore or forget old tweets and not only do people dip in and out of the tweet-stream as the spirit moves them, old tweets are dropped from the Twitter database. Tweets are ephemeral. Blogs, on the other hand, are relatively per-manent and indexed by Google. Opinions expressed and links posted on blogs are findable, readable, and clickable.

Why keep score? If you discover which individuals help you reach the most people, you can target some of your attention to them personally. If you discover which indi-viduals help you reach the most valuable people, you can address this top tier directly, personally, and frequently to keep them talking. You could send them a gift basket, but a better option is to send them exclusive "insider" info to help them be more valuable to their readers and repeaters.

Your message multiplier velocity tells you whether your insight is popular or prosaic by revealing how many people thought your message was worthy of repeating. Then there's its velocity; how quickly the message spread and the scope of its dissemination.

These are essential measures for determining whether you are resonating with your target audience and who within your organization is best equipped to be the face of the firm in the social media spheres. "Influencity," anybody? In his book *Web Analytics 2.0*, Avinash Kaushik describes these as Citations.

Avinash says Citations occur when people comment about your blog posts on their own blogs and uses Techno-rati rank to keep track. Technorati's FAQ describes Authority as "the number of blogs linking to a web site in the last six months. The higher the number, the more Technorati Authority the blog has.... The smaller your Technorati Rank, the closer you are to the top." This is a dynamic number as it can change after every post. So rather than a measurement of readership, this is a measurement of the interest other bloggers have in your blog based on links.

Hubs and Spokes

If you're like me, you'd be willing to trade some of those early Google T-shirts you collected at trade shows for a network map of these connections so you can visualize who the real Influentials are. This is not as easy as Tom Lehrer makes it sound in his viral song from 1980 (www.youtube.com/watch?v=xKZR3Bcj4jw), but it can be done.

The first step is to code the links you publish so that when they are republished and re-re-retweeted, any clicks can be traced back to the original tweet or post. That means a normal link like www.example.com becomes www.example.com? 1234. You can now count the number of times the code 1234 shows up in your analytics database to determine how far-reaching that post or tweet was (Figure 3.1).

Another definition of following the conversation is tracking subject matter. The social graph lets you visualize not just the connection to people but the connection to people along different subject vectors. That helps you identify what parts of your message resonated with which market segments. Not everybody will care that your new car uses parts sourced from Wisconsin but they are interested in the styling, mileage, and engine capacity.

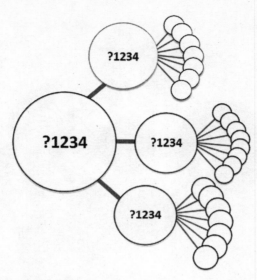

Figure 3.1   Coded links in posts identify the traffic generated by online word-of-mouth.

Subsequent to your automobile launch, Figure 3.2 shows that there is a strong interest in style, but the conversation drops off pretty quickly. Once somebody has seen some photos and passed along the "Did you see this?" message to their friends, the excitement wanes.

Meanwhile, the discussion about horsepower seems to have more horsepower while the mileage discussion is getting a lot of mileage. You now have a clear understanding of what intrigues people most about your new vehicle. You have marketplace insight you can act on. You know how to tweak your tweets.

ARE THEY A LINK TO AN ORTHOGONAL SOCIAL GROUP?

You may also be lucky enough to spark the interest of people you had not targeted. Figure 3.3 shows that the mileage

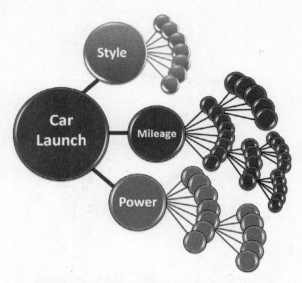

Figure 3.2   Different areas of interest echo
your message to varying degrees.

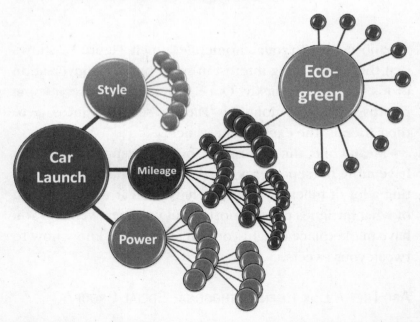

Figure 3.3   This new car announcement generated uninten-
tional excitement in an unexpected area of interest.

discussion ignited a healthy amount of conversation in the environmental population and that caught fire elsewhere.

The good news is that you now have a new audience to engage and a new dialogue to fire up. The seemingly bad news is that you should have known this community of interest would be interested and reached out to them directly. It turns out, reaching them through others is much more powerful. See "Word-of-Mouth Research" below.

Word-of-Mouth Research

EXECUTIVE SUMMARY:

The authors investigate the effectiveness of a firm proactively managing customer-to-customer communication. In particular, they are interested in proving how, if at all, a firm should go about effecting a meaningful word-of-mouth (WOM) communications program. This is done through two different data collection schemes: a large-scale, 15-market test through BzzAgent with a client restaurant chain, and also through a controlled online experiment. The results are somewhat counterintuitive and may change the way web analysts and Marketers should be thinking about WOM and social analysis, particularly if there is a hard monetary investment in the WOM program.

Specially [sic], the researchers are trying to answer 2 questions:

(continued)

(*continued*)

1. What kind of WOM maximizes incremental Sales?

   The answer: WOM created by less loyal (not highly loyal) customers, and occurring between acquaintances (not friends). Though perhaps surprising, this result is often found in Marketing program measurement; Sales would occur anyway without the program, especially among best customers. Said another way, the results demonstrate the pitfalls of not using control groups (people not exposed to the campaign) to accurately measure Marketing effectiveness.

2. Which kinds of people are most effective at creating the WOM above?

   The answer: "Opinion Leaders" or "Fans" are not as effective in spreading WOM that drives incremental Sales because these efforts are "preaching to the choir," per #1 above. The networks that opinion leaders or fans have are likely to already know about the Product from pre-existing conversations, and spending money on creating a campaign to reach these people is ineffective because the social communication has already taken place.

   In sum, if you want to invest in a WOM program that will drive Sales you would not have received anyway, you want the WOM conversations happening, as the authors say, "where none would have naturally occurred otherwise."

> As is typical of academic research and testing, there is an extensive review of the results of other WOM Marketing studies all the way back to the 1970s upon which the hypothesis for this test was formulated.
>
> Analyst and marketing optimization expert Jim Novo's review of "Firm-Created Word-of-Mouth Communication: Evidence from a Field Test," *Marketing Science*, Vol. 28, No. 4, by David Godes and Dina Mayzlin, 2009. Posted on the Web Analytics Association web site at www.webanalyticsassociation.org/en/art/712.

As in every aspect of social media metrics, there are nascent tools offered that try to bring order out of the conversational chaos. FMS Advanced Systems Group's Sentinel Visualizer (Figure 3.4) is one example.

The Sentinel Visualizer claims to answer questions like:

- How highly connected is an entity within a network?
- What is an entity's overall importance in a network?
- How central is an entity within a network?
- How does information flow within a network?

It suggests that you can:

- Identify central players automatically.
- Locate organizational cut-points.
- Perform timeline analysis.

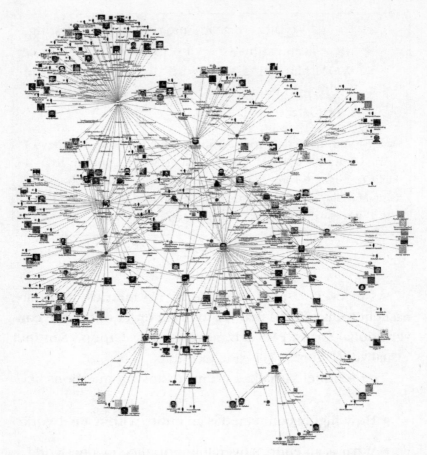

Figure 3.4   The Sentinel Visualizer includes the faces of those talking about a specific subject.

♦ Organize complex data relationships into cells and cliques.

♦ Find all paths, the shortest path, or the best paths between two entities.

Further, Sentinel Visualizer offers a time slider control to see how networks form, change, and interact with each other over time—down to the second. I suppose if you were in a legal battle about who said what to whom first, second-by-second social graphing might just be considered useful. But the purpose of temporal conversation tracking is to spot patterns and predict behavior. It provides insight as to when to release information by day of week and time of day.

ARE THEY JOINED AT THE HIP?

Companies like Axiom (www.axiom.com), Rapleaf (www.rapleaf.com), and Unbound Technologies (www.unboundtech.com) are mapping the relationships in a different way.

Rather than follow conversations, which is tricky at best, these companies scour the social networking sites and blogs for friends and blogrolls. This information is declarative rather than inferred. I am your friend. I include you in my blogroll to indicate that I think your posts are worth reading. This information is there for the taking—it's public.

With this connection information, Axiom can match their own database with yours and report back on which of your customers or prospects is linked to which others. You now know how your community is linked. That is, you know which of those in your database make up a sub-community. That's invaluable for sending targeted messages.

All a-Twitter

Twitter is the current darling of the social media world. Yes, that statement dates this book as written before _____ ? _____ and _____ ? _____ were recognized as the game changers they are. Since I have no powers of clairvoyance, let's explore the variety of ways people are trying to measure influencity with the game changer at hand.

NUMBER OF FOLLOWERS

This one is simple, easy to understand, and already covered as useful to a point, but not indicative of success. It's also easy to accomplish. You can automatically find and follow people who will automatically follow you in return. If all you want is more followers, you can flip that switch but with no residual value.

FOLLOWERS OF FOLLOWERS

If John is followed by 50,000 people who have no followers of their own, he is in a world of hurt compared with Jane, who is followed by 10,000 people who are each followed by 1,000 others. The guarantee of creating an opportunity to see for 50,000 pales next to the opportunity to generate an opportunity to see for 10 million. Even if you assume that only a fraction of them retweet—say 10 percent—you've still reached 1.1 million.

More important, that extra million received a retweet, which is more highly valued by the individual. If you boast about your new car, I absorb the fact of the launch. But if Jane retweets your message, it implies that she thinks it's worthy of my attention, rather than just being a promotion from the manufacturer.

TWEET RECENCY AND FREQUENCY

The more you communicate, the better—to a degree of diminishing returns. We can clearly agree that a spokesperson who tweets twice and the most recent one was a year ago is *not* generating value for the company. But constant, banal chatter is not a plus.

RATIO OF FOLLOWING TO FOLLOWER

Those who measure this sort of thing claim the higher the ratio, the better. If everybody follows you, but you follow only a few, then you must be cool, hip, important? It's a mystery. Does Britney Spears really follow 432,595 people? I guess she has a lot of time on her hands. Does Ellen DeGeneres really follow only 26? Now *they* must be really special. What's the business value of this ratio as a Key Performance Indicator? Beats me.

RETWEETS

This one speaks for itself. If you said something that is worthy of repeating, then you get a gold star. You also get to think long and hard about why your pearls of wisdom were worth repeating. You must have said something that was fun, interesting, or useful, and if you don't know which, you are wasting your time.

Fun and interesting are great for holding the attention of a crowd, but just like funny television ads that you describe to your friends the next day but cannot recall the product, you are not creating value. If everybody remembers Burger King for having the zaniest ads, does that drive food sales? Retweets alone are not going to tell you.

But as metrics that point the way to value generation, retweets beat the heck out of following/follower ratios. Things get interesting, of course, if you layer retweets with who is doing the retweeting. If only those who have three followers are retweeting your pithy prose, then a million retweets will only make you feel good for engaging a high number of low-value people.

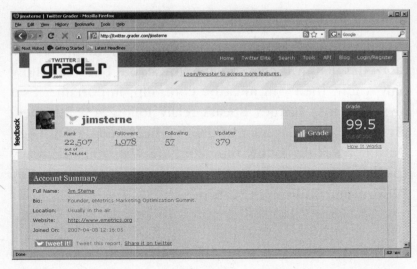

Figure 3.5   A high score feels great, but what does it mean to my business?

Imagine my delight to discover that I scored a 99.5 on Twittergrader.com (Figure 3.5).

Twitter Grader thinks that my measly efforts on Twitter are "better" than 4,721,957 others they are tracking. Only a half a percent of those trackees scored higher than me. It's so tempting to wrestle with a score like that and see what it takes to push it up to 99.6 and then 99.7. But how does that make me a better businessperson? It's a mystery.

Peating the Right Repeater

When you're responsible for promoting a business and meeting business goals, you have to array your resources where you think they are going to be utilized to the best advantage. With infinite resources, you can make sure everybody finds out about your really great products. But infinite resources simply do not exist.

So if you are going to make a concerted effort to reach out to people who can carry your message the best, you have to identify who the Influentials really are on a given topic—your topic. This is where analysis gets interesting and a little murky at the same time.

ARE THEY TOPIC-ORIENTED?

For a while, the hashtag #wa was used to identify tweets about web analytics. A quick trip over to Wefollow.com (Figure 3.6) reveals that there are six people who tweet about #wa more than I do.

If we only consider the top 10 people, there is a clear list of those whom I should contact to spread the word about the eMetrics Marketing Optimization Summit.

Figure 3.6 Wefollow lets you search for people tweeting about your topic and displays their quantity of followers.

They May Be Connected But Are They Respected?

A somewhat disheveled, slightly ragged, unsuccessfully groomed man on a busy street corner waves a large cardboard placard and demands that people wake up to the fact that the sky is falling, the pigeons have stolen his identity, and an envoy from Pluto has taken up residence in his car to plead for its reinstatement as a planet. Everybody within earshot gets the message. Nobody cares. But when E.F. Hutton talks, people listen. So how do you reach the people to whom people actually listen?

The interactive agency Razorfish identified three types of influencers in their 2009 Social Influence Marketing Report called Fluent (http://fluent.razorfish.com/publication/?m=6540&l=1):

> *Key influencers in specific fields have an outsized influence on brand affinity and purchasing decisions on social platforms. Key influencers typically have their own blogs, huge Twitter followings and rarely know their audiences personally.*

Think of this group as journalists. They propound to the masses and amass a critical mass of followers.

> *Social influencers are everyday people who participate in social platforms. These users are typically in your consumer's social graph and influence brand affinity and purchasing decisions through consumer reviews, by updating their own status and Twitter feeds and commenting on blogs and forums. In some cases the consumer knows the social influencers personally.*

These folks like to comment. They love to opine and their opinion is served to all, seen by many, and savored by some.

> ***Known peer influencers*** *are the closest to both the purchasing decision and to the consumer. They are typically family members, or part of the consumer's inner circle. They influence the purchasing decision most directly and have to live with the results of their family member or friend's decision as well.*

This group is very valuable to a decision maker because their opinion is imbued with all the background knowledge of acquaintance.

If Theo thinks this thermos is thoroughbred . . .

If Sally says this software is super . . .

If Gary agrees this garden hose it great . . .

If Frank feels this furniture is faultless . . .

Various people have varying degrees of clout. Sadly, the metrics in play today are all about secondary reach, with a couple of exceptions.

AUTHORITY

The best-known use of "authority" as a social media clout metric is on Technorati. In a blog post about rating blog posts (http://technorati.com/weblog/2007/05/354.html), Technorati founder and Chairman of the Board Dorion Carroll explained it very simply.

Technorati Authority is the number of blogs link-ing to a web site in the last six months. The higher the number, the more Technorati Authority the blog has.

It is important to note that we measure the num-ber of blogs, rather than the number of links. So, if a blog links to your blog many times, it still only counts as +1 toward your authority. Of course, new links mean the +1 will last another 180 days.

The Technorati Top 100 shows the most popular 100 blogs based on Technorati Authority. The #1 ranked blog is the blog with the most other distinct blogs linking to it in the last six months. If your blog's rank is, say 305,316, this indicates that there are 305,315 blog ranks separating your blog from the #1 position.

Google got its start on that premise. The two wunder-kind founders were trying to come up with some way to better identify relevance than Yahoo! and utilized the cita-tion model. If others cite your peer-reviewed paper, then it must be a good paper. If lots of people link to your web site using that particular word or phrase as the anchor text, your web site must be about that particular word or phrase.

Retweetrank (www.retweetrank.com) ranks Twitter users for how often they are retweeted. Lunch menus do not score high.

Impact

Authority is based on the number of people who point to you as a reference. But with the advent of Twitter, other tools arrived with other definitions.

Figure 3.7   Eric T. Peterson's own score on his own Twitter analysis tool.

Eric T. Peterson of Web Analytics Demystified is a web analytics thought leader of the first order. He was one of the first to tap the Twitter API and created Twitalyzer (Figure 3.7).

Twitalyzer looks at each five dimensions of each Twitter account: Influence, Signal, Generosity, Velocity, and Clout.

Influence is a culmination of some of the others, so we'll circle back to that one.

SIGNAL-TO-NOISE RATIO

Hinged on the opinion that "people tend to gravitate towards strangers who are passing along information," Twitalyzer's signal-to-noise ratio measures how much an individual passes along facts rather than anecdotes. It seems impossibly aspirational until you look at the rather straight-forward criteria. Your tweet is considered signal as opposed to noise if you:

- ◆ Reference other people (use of "@" followed by text).

- ◆ Include a URL (use of "http://" followed by text).

- ◆ Include hashtags (use of "#" followed by text).

- ◆ Retweet others (use of "rt," "r/t/," "retweet," or "via").

By this measure, Eric is short on stories about his cat and long on signal-rich tweets.

GENEROSITY

Being generous in this context relates to your willingness to pass along what others have tweeted—the retweet. If your tweets are all about you all the time, your score drops. If you only retweet others, your score hits 100. While it seems odd that somebody who posts nothing original scores the highest, this metric serves as a function of overall influence rather than a goal unto itself. Nevertheless, if you're really good at finding great stuff to repeat you will indeed build a brand and grow an audience.

VELOCITY

Most would assume that the term *velocity* applies better to a metric for an individual tweet or even a meme as it rock-ets around the interconnected online world. To Twitalyzer, "velocity" is a measure of how much you tweet. Think of this as output. You tweet a lot? You score higher. While this metric is easy to hit, it is limited by the harm done to your brand. As Eric puts it, "Twittering a lot about nothing will increase your velocity but decrease your signal-to-noise ratio. And while the latter is not directly factored into the influence calculation at Twitalyzer, in our experience if you start to ramble about nothing you will lose followers very, very quickly."

CLOUT

This one is simple: the number of times @you are mentioned by others. It is formally "the number of references to you divided by the total number of possible references (as governed by the Twitter Search APIs)."

Now it's time to roll all of these into one.

INFLUENCE

The number of people who follow you is just one piece of influence in Twitalyzer's book. It measures your overall influence based on:

♦ Your relative reach in Twitter, measured by the number of followers you have.

♦ Your relative authority, measured by the number of times you are "retweeted."

♦ Your relative generosity, measured by the number of times you "retweet" others.

♦ Your relative clout, measured by the number of times you are referenced by others.

♦ Your relative velocity, measured by the number of updates you publish over a seven-day period.

All told, Twitalyzer scores your Twitter "goodness." It's a way to keep tabs on your efforts or the efforts of the many people tweeting on behalf of your company. Using these scores, you can keep your finger on their pulse and compare them with the tweets of competitors.

PostRank (www.postrank.com) is a scoring system that ranks "any kind of online content, such as RSS feed items, blog posts, articles, or news stories." PostRank defines social engagement as how interesting or relevant people have found an item or category. "Examples of engagement include writing a blog post in response to someone else, bookmarking an article, leaving a comment on a blog, or clicking a link to read a news item. . . . The more interesting or relevant an item is, the more work they will do to share or respond to that item so interactions that require more effort are weighted higher."

There are many other tools popping up that attempt to identify who are the most influential people on Twitter for any given category, subject matter, or brand. These are highly desired for figuring out whom to target and how to express yourself in such a way as to catch their attention.

But so far, they are opportunistic at best. They latch on to the data that's available and try to make it mean something, rather than apply rigor in scientific study. A bit like seeking patterns in tea leaves, head bumps, and lines on one's palm. Interesting and thought provoking, but not clearly identifying business value.

The Problem of Fish and the Pond

Suresh Vittal makes a very compelling argument for getting a handle on context in all things at all times. Suresh is a principal analyst at Forrester Research whose research agenda includes:

♦ Enterprise marketing technologies,

♦ Database marketing strategies,

♦ Customer analytics, and

♦ Technologies that make customer insight operational.

He says it's good to know if the individual influencer you are tracking is a valuable member of a network. "But how valuable is that network?" he asks. "Authority tells you how influential this individual is and how much influence this person wields over his or her network. But frankly if the network isn't very valuable, should you assign the same degree of importance to this individual's influence as you would somebody else?"

It's a problem of a heavy hitter with a very loud voice in a very small pond or a very loud voice in completely the wrong pond. "Or" he flips the argument back on its head, "a very loud voice in a very small pond happens to include one or more really big fish.

"You need to take into context the tone and the relevance, the authority and the value of that overall network to your brand when assigning influence. A few tools, if any, allow you to do all of this."

The Empty Metric

The underlying problem with measuring how much a person talks or how many people talk about a given subject is that you can only tell that they are talking and what they are talking about. You just don't know how they feel.

In Hollywood, Oscar Wilde is right. The only thing worse than people talking about you is people not talking about you. In Hollywood, there's no such thing as bad press. In business, talking is good only if they are saying good things about you.

CHAPTER 4
Getting Emotional—
Recognizing Sentiment

"The meaning coded into words can't be measured in bytes. It's deeply compressed. Twelve words from Voltaire can hold a lifetime of experience."
— *Mark Horowitz, "Visualizing Big Data." Wired,*
June 23, 2008.
www.wired.com/science/discoveries/magazine/
16-07/pb_visualizing

It's great that your name is being mentioned by friends and fans but it's also being mentioned by those who are neither. It's your job to note if those people are saying sad things, mad things, or bad things. It's your job to listen and respond and hopefully change their mind and change their tune.

It would be better if they repeat and reinforce those characteristics you want them to associate with your brand and your products. It would be nice if they propagate the notion that your company stands for luxury, value, quality, excitement, status, or fun. You pray that you can change their dissatisfaction to support.

Wouldn't it be nice if they were talking about you in the glowing terms enjoyed by brands like Apple, Harley-Davidson, and Disney? Wouldn't it be nice if they were advocating your goods and services to others? It's more important than nice—it's critical. People believe other people far more than they believe the one selling the snake oil.

My Brother Doug's Shirts

Humans are emotional creatures. We pay attention to the emotions of other humans. We respond in terms of flight, flight, or mate. Everything else is psycho- and social-conditioning cobbled on top so we can get along better in ever-increasing numbers in ever-decreasing spaces.

The marketing professional is tasked with tapping into this lizard-brain, gut-reaction, psychological quagmire and captivating us through their powers of persuasion. Some have gotten very good at it. Some have used higher-order statistical analytics to target us with just the right message at just the right time. But they can't compete with my brother Doug.

The most compelling discount offer, the most heartfelt celebrity endorsement or the most powerful, massive, and expensive marketing campaign cannot survive an ever-so-slight frown on my brother Doug's face when I'm shopping for dress shirts.

Doug has exquisite taste in dress shirts. On the one hand this is a shame as I've seen some really great shirts I wanted to get him as gifts but simply would not presume to choose on his behalf. He has style, he has taste, and he dresses in an elegantly casual way that communicates breeding and panache without any pomposity or arrogance whatsoever. Sartorially speaking, if Doug says it's good, it's golden. Whether he tells me his feelings over lunch, on the phone, or in an e-mail, I pay close attention.

But when it comes to deciding on a refrigerator, a new laptop, or a flea-repelling, coat-glossening, good-smelling dog shampoo that won't irritate delicate skin, Doug is not the first person I turn to. Instead, I turn to the "wisdom of the crowds."

How much do we listen to others' opinions? Here are just a few tidbits from Bazaarvoice's long list of examples of the power of word-of-mouth and consumer demand for ratings and reviews at www.bazaarvoice.com/resources/stats:

♦ "Person like me" is still the most trusted source for information about a company and, therefore, products. (Edelman Trust Barometer, November 2007)

♦ Recommendations from family and friends trump all other consumer touchpoints when it comes to influencing purchases, according to ZenithOptimedia. (AdAge, April, 2008)

♦ Recommendation is the number-one reason for choosing a particular site. (Royal Mail's Home Shopping Tracker Study, September 2007)

♦ Users who contribute product reviews or post messages visit sites nine times as often as noncontributors do. Contributors also make purchases nearly twice as often. (McKinsey & Co./Jupiter Media Metrix study, January 2002)

♦ Review users noted that reviews generated by fellow consumers had a greater influence than those generated by professionals. (comScore/The Kelsey Group, October 2007)

The great unwashed masses are pouring out their hearts onto the great unwashed canvas of the Internet. Their opinions about absolutely everything, including your company, your products, and your employees are laid bare for all to see. You should take a look. Some companies are getting serious about it.

In "Tracking the Influence of Conversations: A Roundtable Discussion on Social Media Metrics and Measurement, A Dow Jones White Paper," Ed Terpening, blogging projects manager at Wells Fargo, said:

> *We care a lot about participation and engagement. That's our No. one metric. But when we're using social media as a research vehicle, then it's sentiment and opinion—the quality of what people are saying about the brand, what words they're associating with the brand.*

Tell Us How You Really Feel

Ever been in a crowd and heard somebody say your first name out loud? Gets your attention, doesn't it? Next time you're in a large group like a sporting event, stand up and shout "Mike!" or "Susan!" and see how many heads swivel your way.

Now think back to when you were about 10 years old and you heard your mother calling your name. There were several distinct messages she was able to convey in just two syllables, especially if your name was only one syllable:

♦ It's dinnertime.

♦ It's bedtime.

- Your great aunt Bertha is here and we all have to be on our best behavior.

- Turn that TV off this instant.

- I've fallen and I can't get up.

- I just discovered those cigarettes in your sock drawer and you're really going to get it now and I mean how!

How did you know what she was thinking? You just did. It's a gift.

Ever have a misunderstanding with somebody? They said one thing and you thought they said another? Ever had something lost in translation? Now take away the body language, the vocal mannerisms and inflections, and the temporal context. What have you got? Raw text.

In a *New York Times* article called "Mining the Web for Feelings, Not Facts" (August 24, 2009, www.nytimes.com/2009/08/24/technology/internet/24emotion.html), Alex Wright put it this way:

> *The practical side of this is technically challenging. Again and again, we face the conflict between human communication norms and computer processing limitations. It takes a person to understand a person—and even then it's easy to misunderstand.*

I had an eye-opening conversation with a marketing manager from Microsoft after their launch of Office 2000. She was very excited about a new feature they were trying on their web site for customer feedback. Instead of a Feedback button that went to a generic form, they added a free-form text box to the bottom of every article they added to the web site. They asked people to tell them if the article was helpful or not and what else they had been looking for.

"Interesting," said I, thinking this was a great way to listen to customers. "How's that working out? Are people willing to communicate that way? Are you learning lots?"

"Yes and no," she said.

"Oh? People aren't articulate?"

"Oh, they communicate surprisingly well."

"How many responses do you get?"

"Somewhere between five and 10 per day."

"So you're not learning much because...."

"Five or 10 per day—on each article."

"Uh huh ..."

"We have over 10,000 articles."

"Oh," I said eloquently. "So, how are you managing? What are you doing?"

"We're looking into textual analysis tools."

Sentimental Journey—a Framework

In order to parse out and measure human emotional communication or "subjective information extraction," it helps to have a color chart and a thermometer.

The color chart is there to determine if the outburst is green, red, or gray (positive, negative, or neutral), and the thermometer tells you if the outburster is objectively subjective or foaming at the mouth. The color chart is known as polarity and the thermometer measures intensity.

Polarity

The pot roast is in the oven.
    Neutral.

The pot roast is delicious.
> Positive.

The pot roast is the worst I've ever tasted.
> Negative.

The pot roast is inedible.
> Oooo. Hard to say. It might just be a statement of fact.

The pot roast is better than your mother's.
> Damning with faint praise?

As Seth Grimes from consulting firm Alta Plana put it in that August 24, 2009, *New York Times* article, "Sentiments are very different from conventional facts... 'Sinful' is a good thing when applied to chocolate cake."

Sarcasm, irony, idioms, slang, and the common language that crops up and fades away are all nemeses of a programmatic algorithm designed to classify emotion. And that's only a part of the problem.

Intensity

"I hate this!" she said quietly.
> The agony of waiting for a dental appointment.

"I hate this!" she said laughing.
> She actually liked being tickled.

"I hate this!" she said petulantly.
> Her older sister gets to go out and she has to stay home.

"I hate this!" she said vehemently.
> The incessant arguing is pushing her over the brink.

Intensity is about the degree of emotion, something a person can pick up pretty quick in person but makes communicating by e-mail trickier—hence emoticons.

How did the author actually feel? How do you tell?

Those who try to programmatically classify emotional statements look for clues wherever they can find them. More adjectives might mean more opinion. Lots of nouns and verbs suggests objectivity. Exclamation points are sometimes useful. It's tricky.

And, of course, it depends on who's doing the talking.

SOURCES AND TARGETS

Whose opinion is—about whom?

If Henry complains about everything, then what Henry has to say about your products has to be taken with a fairly good sized grain of salt. What Fox News says about Democrats or MSNBC says about Republicans must be strained through a fine-mesh filter. And don't get me started about health care!

In their paper "Toward Opinion Summarization: Linking the Sources" (www.cs.cornell.edu/home/cardie/papers/acl2006ws.pdf), Veselin Stoyanov and Claire Cardie from Cornell University spell it out this way:

> *Several research efforts (e.g. Riloff and Wiebe (2003), Bethard et al. (2004), Wilson et al. (2004), Yu and Hatzivassiloglou (2003), Wiebe and Riloff (2005)) have shown that sentiment information can be extracted at the sentence, clause, or individual opinion expression level (fine-grained opinion information). However, little has been done to develop methods for combining*

*fine-grained opinion information to form a sum-
mary representation in which expressions of
opinions from the same source/target are grouped
together, multiple opinions from a source toward
the same target are accumulated into an aggre-
gated opinion, and cumulative statistics are
computed for each source/target.*

Yes, we're still learning. It's early days. If you're captivated by how human communication can be captured
and deciphered, I suggest "Opinion Mining and Sentiment Analysis" by Bo Pang and Lillian Lee (www.cs.
cornell.edu/home/llee/omsa/omsa-published.pdf).

But isn't there enough technology out there somewhere
that can pull all the bits and pieces together?

The Promise of Automated Understanding

There have long been text analysis tools that focus on
unstructured data like documents, spreadsheets, and survey
results. Used primarily as search tools, they are now being
trained on the ocean of emotion called the social media
space.

Analyzing the outpouring of millions of souls can reveal
attitudinal shifts that are not visible to opinion polls, survey takers, or customer satisfaction questionnaires. Tracking
public sentiment over time provides invaluable insight and
gives you the chance to stay right on top of changes in the
marketplace and your organization's brand equity.

Social media–specific number crunchers are popping
up all the time but as of this writing, they are immature
curiosities rather than serious business tools.

Chris Near, director of research at KDPaine & Partners, is no newcomer to measuring public opinion and the impact of PR campaigns. In a blog post in May 2009 (www.themeasurementstandard.com/issues/5-1-09/neartwittersentiment5-1-09.asp) he wrote, "When my company, KDPaine & Partners, wants to do very accurate measurement of Twitter, we have to use human readers. It's the only way to really understand the language."

Chris went on to describe five different tools that, he said "have their own set of problems." Their names have changed by now, the feature sets will have become richer, or they will have disappeared altogether. But the problems remain. In an ideal world, the ideal Twitter analysis tool would include:

♦ The ability to search by any word, abbreviation, symbol, or emoticon that would ever occur in a tweet.

♦ Advanced search features, including by date, by user, by hashtag, and by tone.

♦ The ability to distinguish between posts from a person/company, posts to a person/company, and posts referencing a person/company.

♦ Results charts with colors that distinguish between different sentiments.

♦ A dashboard with quick totals for each tone type, as well as overall numbers/percentages.

♦ The ability to search over long periods of time.

♦ Instant charts to show trends and relevant occurrences.

♦ At least 80 percent accuracy. 90 percent to 95 percent would be better.

♦ Real-time updates.

♦ No cost. (That's not too much to ask, is it?)

Sadly, according to Chris, "None of the tools reviewed . . . come even close to meeting this wish list. But some are on the right track."

The main issue is that sentiment as it is commonly practiced today is based on the "bag of words" approach to parsing. If they include the words "hate" or "bad" or "ridiculous," then it must be negative.

The developers of Twittratr.com call it a StartupWeekend project. "We built a list of positive keywords and a list of negative keywords. We search Twitter for a keyword and the results we get back are crossreferenced against our adjective lists, then displayed accordingly. There are obvious issues with this, so if you have any ideas on how we could do this better let us know."

In this era of transparency, they posted their lists on Google Docs for all to review. Their lists are prosaic. As you can see from the examples taken from the positive and negative lists (Table 4.1), there are many combinations of words from both columns that might confuse and confound Twittratr.

The bag-of-words approach is viable when sifting through petabytes of documents, trying to decipher *what* each one is about. Pure statistical engines compare and contrast the frequency of specific words in a document against the frequency of those words in all other documents. But if your entire document is 140 characters, that method just doesn't have enough grist for the mill.

Table 4.1 Twittratr.com uses these and more in their bag-of-words to rate tweets for sentiment

Specific Sentiment Words from Twittratr.com	
Positive Words	**Negative Words**
http://docs.google.com/Doc?id =df5m8zwp_92gvtfm3d9	http://docs.google.com/Doc?id =df5m8zwp_93gd2mhkd7
Woo	irritating
quite amazing	not that good
looking forward to	suck
damn good	lying
frickin ruled	duplicity
frickin rules	angered
way to go	dumbfounding
cute	dumbifying
comeback	not as good
not suck	not impressed
prop	stomach it
kinda impressed	pw
props	pwns
come on	pwnd
congratulation	pwning
gtd	in a bad way
proud	horrifying
thanks	wrong
can help	failing
thanks!	fallen way behind
pumped	fallen behind
integrate	lose
really like	fallen
loves it	self-deprecating
yay	hunker down
amazing	duh
epic flail	got killed by
flail	hated us
good luck	only works in safari
fail	must have ie
life saver	fuming and frothing

piece of cake	heavy
good thing	buggy
hawt	unusable
hawtness	nothing is
highly positive	is great until
my hero	don't support
LOL	despise
:)	sucks
;)	problems
:-)	not working
;-)	fuming
:D	an issue
;]	WTF
:]	:(
:p	:-(
;p	

Even when we have enough grist, suggesting that every statement that includes the phrase "is a great deal" is necessarily positive is going to lead us into trouble. As humans, we can instantly classify these three examples from Lillian Lee (www.cs.cornell.edu/home/llee/talks/llee-aaai08.pdf):

1. This laptop is a great deal.

2. A great deal of media attention surrounded the release of the new laptop.

3. This laptop is a great deal . . . and I've got a nice bridge you might be interested in.

Perhaps machines can eventually be taught. But who will teach them? Machines have such a hard time with this because humans do, too.

What We Have Here Is a Failure to Communicate—How Sad is That?

In some very straightforward research documented in a very straightforward paper called "Detecting Sadness in 140 Characters: Sentiment Analysis and Mourning Michael Jackson on Twitter," Elsa Kim and Sam Gilbert et al. proved that this is too hard even for humans.

The task was basic:

> *Michael Jackson's death created an emotional outpouring of unprecedented magnitude on Twitter. In this report, we examine 1,860,427 tweets about Jackson's death in order to test various methods of sentiment analysis and gain insights into how people express emotion on Twitter.*

They wanted to know if tweets about Michael Jackson that included the word "sad" were really expressing sadness about Michael Jackson's passing. Sounds a bit simplistic, right? Hold on to your socks.

First, they took 44,383 tweets and analyzed them against the ANEW dataset.

> *The Affective Norms for English Words (ANEW) dataset contains normative emotional ratings for 1034 English words. Each word in the dataset is associated with a rating of 1–9 along each of three dimensions of emotional affect: valence (pleasure vs. displeasure), arousal (excitement vs. calmness), and dominance (strength vs. weakness)* (Bradley and Lang, 1999).

The scoring of the tweets along those dimensions is documented in this 15-page PDF but it wasn't the red flashing light for me. That came when they then randomly selected 346 tweets and asked six human coders to sort them. The coders were asked to tag each one:

♦ "Y"—yes; the person who created this tweet is expressing sadness

♦ "N"—no; the person who created this tweet is not expressing sadness

♦ "M"—mixed; the person who created this tweet expresses sadness as well as another conflicting emotion

♦ "U"—unclear; the tweet in question is spam, is not in English, or is otherwise impossible to interpret with respect to sentiment.

How do you use the word "sad" in a way that does not express sadness? Turns out to be easy. Let's start with calm and sad:

"Michael Jackson's death is a sad loss . . . thoughts and prayers go out to his family."

Next, hyperemotional:

"Michael Jackson Died!! whatt??? im saddened . . . deeply sad:("

Then, sad about the results:

"Saddened and unsurprised watching the prices change on Michael Jackson CDs in second hand shops."

And sad about something else:

"Who'da thunk that today would be the day that Michael Jackson died? It feels fake. I'm SO sad about Farrah Fawcett. Such a surreal day . . ."

And:

"TMZ.com claims that Michael Jackson is dead, but his Wikipedia page has yet to be updated. How sad is it that I went to Wikipedia?"

Not to mention spam:

"RT @bowlsey @JamieC: Very sad about Michael Jackson. HABITAT—for all your furniture needs—habitat.co.uk."

The red-flashing-light clue is right up front in the Key Findings section where they say, "Roughly $\frac{3}{4}$ of tweets about Jackson's death that use the word 'sad' actually express sadness, suggesting that sentiment analysis based on word usage is fairly accurate."

In other words, using a brute-force bag-of-words approach to determining sentiment is wrong 25 percent of the time and this *is considered fairly accurate.* Yes—it gets better. None of the people rating the tweets found any to be mixed and yet:

All six raters agreed on only 235 (67.92 percent) tweets.

How on earth is a machine going to label something as seemingly simple as sadness when humans can't agree?

Rather than throw their hands up in the air and give up, some are asking the man and machine to work together. Turns out machines can learn from people.

Hope on the Horizon

One of the tenets of artificial intelligence is that the machine can learn from its mistakes without having to be told what the mistake was. It *does*, however, need to be told that a mistake was made.

Over time, it assigns enough mathematical values to a wider variety of mistakes and makes probability evaluations to determine future decisions.

So what would happen if Kim and Gilbert's test were not a one-time consideration but an ongoing collaboration? What if humans looked over the results and directed the machine, like an adult would for a child?

In the world of weekend application development, that's the same approach that Twitter Sentiment tried (http://twittersentiment.appspot.com). The first thing to love about Twitter Sentiment is that the copyright mark on the home page is 2020. That made me smile. I also smiled at the complete write-up the developers provided in their *Twitter Sentiment Analysis* paper

Alec Go (alecmgo@stanford.edu)

Lei Huang (leirocky@stanford.edu)

Richa Bhayani (richab86@stanford.edu)

CS224N—Final Project Report

June 6, 2009, 5:00 P.M. (3 Late Days)

http://nlp.stanford.edu/courses/cs224n/2009/fp/3.pdf

But the thing I really liked was that they reach out to humans to help teach the machine. The very first tweet listed is color coded as negative (Figure 4.1), but the machine is wrong.

It's understandable from a bag-of-words perspective. The words "poor" and "losing" are pretty strong. But the tweet is using them about the Bears and not the Tigers. This is a very positive tweet about the Tigers.

So, I use my powers of human intellect and mouse control to reverse the polarity Twitter Sentiment on that Tweet (Figure 4.2).

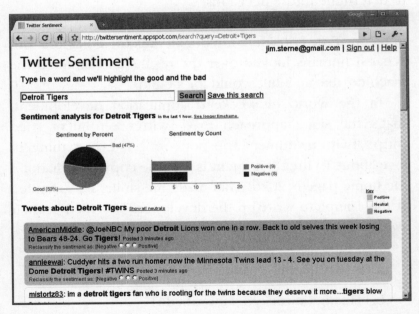

Figure 4.1 Twitter Sentiment invites humans to help teach their software about polarity.

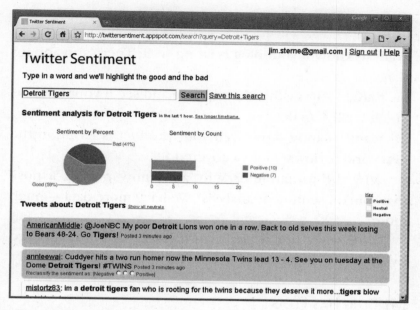

Figure 4.2 With nothing more than manual dexterity, I have shifted the communal sentiment about the Detroit Tigers by 6 percent.

I'm still wondering how this tweet got classified as negative:

Chicago_SC: Sox lose 5-3 to **Tigers** in finale Sorry Chicago! I LOVES MY **TIGERS**! GO **DETROIT**! (via @LAScooterGirls) http://twitpic.com/ka9eq

But now it's time to get serious. The team that created Twitter Sentiment say that it "is strictly a school project." So what's a business to do? It's time to turn our attention to some of the more serious sentiment analysis services.

Sentiment Beyond Twitter

Want to know if your blog is faring well? There's an app for that.

Care to survey the blogosphere and see if your brand is doing well? Can do.

Want to know how well your product is faring in the news and reviews? Got ya covered.

Why the turnaround? Why am I now putting a positive spin on sentiment analysis? We have more data—much more.

Once we're free of the 140-character stricture imposed by Twitter, sentiment is easier to recognize mathematically.

MY BLOG HAS FLEAS

Is your blog well received? Social Mention (www .socialmention.com) includes a "sentiment" rating that they simply describe as "the ratio of mentions that are generally positive to those that are generally negative without much of a clue about how they determine it. But if you, like Eric T. Peterson (Figure 4.3), score 20 positives to 1 negative, chances are you're doing something right.

If you then broaden your horizons beyond blogs to include articles and other publications, you find that classic text mining has been a boon to companies for years.

LISTENING TO THE CHATTER

Yes, that's what the Department of Homeland Security is all about—listening to all the conversations all the time. Now we can listen in for comments about brand affinity and purchase intent, rather than terrorist activity with evil intent.

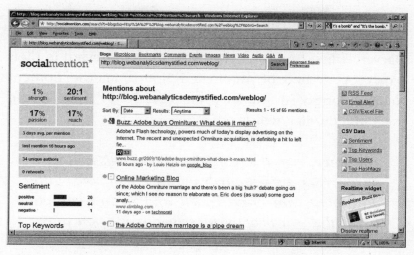

Figure 4.3   Social Mention measures the usual quantity of posts, readers, and comments and then includes a sentiment ratio.

The scientists at Attensity (www.attensity.com) take the same view that man and machine must learn to get along and learn together:

> *Artificial intelligence enables applications to learn from user interactions and the data. For example, if a user marks a response to a customer inquiry as the most accurate response, the system will know to use that response when answering similar inquiries in the future. In essence, the system actually learns from the data that is put into it and the response the business user has to the data.*

Margaret Francis, vice president for product at Scout Labs (www.scoutlabs.com), also appeared in the aforementioned *New York Times* article and crowed, "Our algorithm is about 70 to 80 percent accurate," and explained that users can do the same sort of reclassification to teach the system.

How much human guidance is needed? That's just what Georgetown University Assistant Daniel Hopkins and Harvard University Professor Gary King addressed in their paper "A Method of Automated Nonparametric Content Analysis for Social Science" (June 29, 2009) (http://gking .harvard.edu/files/words.pdf).

Efficiency, as well as confidence intervals and standard errors, are primarily a function of how many documents are hand coded and so are entirely under the control of the investigator. But how many is enough? Hand coding is expensive and time consuming and so we would want to limit its use as much as possible, subject to acceptable uncertainty intervals.

To study this question, we set aside bias by randomly sampling the labeled set directly from the population and plotting . . . the root mean square error (RMSE) averaged across the categories vertically by the number of hand coded documents horizontally for our estimator (straight line) and the direct sampling estimator (dashed line).

For our estimator, the RMSE drops quickly as the number of hand coded documents increase. Even the highest RMSE, with only 100 documents in the labeled set, is only slightly higher than 3 percentage points, which would be acceptable for some applications. (For example, most national surveys have a margin of error of at least 4 percentage points, even when assuming random sampling and excluding all other sources of error.) At about 500 documents, the advantage of more hand coding begins to suffer diminishing returns. In part this is because there is little more error to eliminate as our estimator then has an average RMSE of only about 1.5 percentage points.

The conclusion here is clear: coding more than about 500 documents to estimate a specific quantity of interest is probably not necessary, unless one is interested in much more narrow confidence intervals than is common or in specific categories that happen to be rare. For some applications, as few as 100 documents may even be sufficient.

So are we on the right track putting humans and computers together? Is cyborg sentiment analysis the way to go?

Manya Mayes, SAS chief text mining strategist, says we're already there. Here's an excerpt from her blog from June 11, 2009 (http://blogs.sas.com/text-mining/index. php?/archives/32-Sentiment-Analysis-Overview.html).

I'm going make [sic] a bold statement here— automated sentiment analysis using the right methodology–is actually superior to human sentiment analysis. Bear with me and read through.

The available approaches to analyzing sentiment/satisfaction vary based on the data provided. I would categorize the approaches based on the availability of three types of data:

1. *Customer feedback (free-form text) with customer ranked satisfaction (discrete value), like Amazon product reviews.*

2. *Customer feedback (free-form text) with manually ranked satisfaction (discrete value), where human readers subjectively score the content.*

3. *Customer feedback only, no ranked satisfaction, as with blog posts and comments.*

For the first data type, machine learning algorithms do a good job of measuring overall sentiment (say, +ve/neutral/−ve). Examples of data suitable for this approach are: survey data and product review forums. The problem is that not a lot of text is gathered this way (with a purpose in mind). Even if it is, the machine learning algorithms struggle with distinguishing positive elements from negative. It's one thing to know if a customer is dissatisfied, it is another to know about what!

Given no customer ranked satisfaction, it is possible to build a statistical model using a sample of manually ranked documents, then automatically score the remaining unranked documents. Not many companies are willing to do this. It also doesn't truly represent the customer's opinion—just the reader's interpretation of what the customer thinks.

For the third option, customer opinion with no ranking, you can derive sentiment from the context of the text using natural language processing or NLP. This data is most common and hence so are the approaches to analyzing it. It's not easy, but it's the sweet spot for gain value from the massive volumes of consumer generated text.

One widely available, cheap technology assigns an overall positive or negative sentiment based on assigning positive or negative values to individual words then summing them to get an overall sentiment rating. This approach fails in situations like the following:

♦ *"It's not bad" (two negatives that actually suggest a positive)*

♦ *"I'm not going to say this sucks" (sarcasm or humor)*

♦ *"The keyboard is impossibly small but the display is the best I've seen." (combination)*

The most recent advances in sentiment analysis technology use a combination of techniques:

♦ *Statistics*

♦ *Rule-based definitions and*

♦ *Human intervention, e.g. a final review of the machine scoring.*

The results are less expensive than human-only sentiment analysis, but more consistent. Why? Because the automation adds consistency, while the human verifies the result. When put in the right workflow then it clearly increases scalability by a substantial factor.

We still have trouble telling the difference between "It's a bomb" and "It's the bomb." The important thing about sentiment analysis is that it is a more direct window into the hearts and minds of the marketplace. It is the actual pulse of opinion whether it's about your brand, your industry, or your latest viral video.

We're still at the beginning of using natural language processing, computational linguistics, and artificial intelligence to reveal the sentiment of the public as it changes from day-to-day. The tools and their makers are learning. They will improve in time. Until then, the trends they reveal, while not necessarily precise, are certainly indicative and may be compelling.

Forrester Research's Suresh Vittal thinks our expectations are too high. "I think we're giving it too much of a bad name. I think marketers should stop viewing sentiment analysis as a silver bullet. View it as a great directional tool. View it as something that builds the foundation of customer attitudes and preferences that the marketer has to refine on a periodic basis. The system applies his logic as a business rule on top of it's analytical system and refines sentiment for future posts and conversations.

"There's a great deal of truth and the issues about sarcasm, irony, colloquialism and jargon are serious but it's better to have a system at about 70% accuracy than what we have previously, which was no clue, right?"

At Omniture, a company that sells an enterprise-level marketing management and optimization suite, Matt Langie, senior director of product marketing, agrees with Suresh that our expectations of our ability to programmatically determine sentiment are too high. "Being able to filter tweets for specific keywords such as a phrase or a company or a product name is very straightforward. We'll follow everybody mentioning our Omniture Discover product and we'll aggregate those and label them brand neutral, brand advocates, and brand detractors. Obviously, that's ineffective when someone says, 'This is a terribly good product.'"

While Matt agrees that "there are really no natural language searches that are 100 percent effective," he points out something that people obsessed by the numbers often forget: "You don't need absolute specifics. It's the trends that matter and they are directional. Are your brand advocates increasing faster than your brand detractors?"

So they're out there talking about you.

So they're out there emoting about you.

So what?

Is it causing a reaction of any kind?

CHAPTER 5
Getting Response—Triggering Action

If they read it, repeat it, and like it a lot, you're only part of the way home. Tracking the variations in brand affection in the hearts and minds of the public is good. Knowing if their hearts are glowing or growling is important. But measuring the results your social media efforts engender is vital.

"The More the Merrier" is a fallacy in a networked world. Oh, yes—more is good. But simply having more friends and followers than your competitor is not the best possible measure of a campaign or a brand. More is not an end unto itself—it is a means to an end.

Counting people who follow you and subscribe to your blog and your newsletter is very straightforward. The tricky part is measuring how many of them are actually engaged. (See box below).

Engagement

There are many definitions of engagement and I subscribe to erring on the side of simplicity. When you come across this word in this book, my meaning is not a

(continued)

(*continued*)

formula but only this: *Engagement is when somebody cares and interacts*. And both are necessary.

You can interact with videos, games, jokes, the weather, etc. and not really care about the brand. If you do it enough, you may grow an affection for the brand, but you wouldn't go out of your way to hunt it down if it changed its name and left no forwarding address.

Alternatively, you may think the world of Rolls-Royce cars. You may decide that you have really arrived if and when you can park a Silver Shadow in your driveway. However, you have no intention of buying one. Your daydream is idling by the curb. You don't visit the web site, go out of your way to read articles, or look at pictures of them. You just think it's the bee's knees. Your brand affinity is high but your interaction is low. Therefore, you are not engaged.

How many people think what you have to say is important? Active participation is a much more rational metric than the number of glazed eyeballs that had an opportunity to see but may not have been open when your message was visible.

How Many Made a Note of Your Post?

It's one thing to mention you in their own space—posting your name on their blog, tweeting it to their tweeple, etc., but it's a sign of deeper respect, affinity, and yes, engagement if they are willing to indicate their liking for your company, goods, and/or services on a public web site. Beyond wearing your corporate logo on their polo shirt, posting their linking in a public place is more like a small love note on the bulletin board at the grocery store. It's permanent. It's in front of a lot more people than just their personal friends.

ARE YOU NOTEWORTHY?

Digg, Reddit, Delicious, Stumbleupon, and the like are the hubs for one-click marks of approval. If something you articulate is interesting enough, people will deem it noteworthy—literally noting it on those sites.

As of this writing, the Web Analytics Association is creating a Social Media Standards document that includes this description of a social bookmark:

> *A Social Bookmark is a reference to a URL that is stored, shared, and/or retrieved online. A traditional bookmark is stored on a local browser, while a social bookmark is available online. Social bookmarks are typically seen as a subcategory of your Referrers when analyzing inbound traffic to a web site.*

The metrics here are refreshingly simple.

♦ How many shared a link to your content?

♦ How many links have been shared?

♦ How many people clicked through to it in a given time span?

Web analytics tools and the bookmark services themselves provide useful numbers. Your job is to track how well you're getting this kind of attention and implementing a process for testing and measuring what types of content yield the best results.

The communications staff at Missouri University of Science and Technology use Delicious.com to keep track of online news stories and blog posts to measure the effectiveness of their public relations efforts. In April 2008, Andrew Careaga recounted an example on his blog: Higher Ed Marketing (http://highered.prblogs.org/2008/04/23/delicious-as-a-pr-measurement-tool/).

> *Last week, when the earthquake hit the Midwest, we touted one of our quake experts (J. David Rogers, the Hasselmann Chair of Geological Engineering) to the media. He spoke to 15 different media outlets that Friday, most of them from the Midwest but including our state's two largest daily newspapers and a couple of TV and news radio stations. But none of the stories were saved by other del.icio.us users except for a LiveScience.com story that quoted Rogers and appeared on Yahoo! News. Now we know that 10 other del.icio.us users also saved that story. We also can find out who those users are and what else they're interested in.*
>
> *Another recent news release—about some research on biodegradable plastics bags—got picked up by* Popular Science *magazine's blog PopSci.com, and that also was saved by 10 other users. Another popular sci/tech blog, Gizmodo, picked up the story, and although no other del.icio.us users have saved it, a quick look at the comments shows a high level of interest among Gizmodo readers.*

Leon Hudson commented on Andrew's blog with a reminder that there are subject- and geo-specific bookmarking and news sites to watch as well: "I work for Chong Newztel, a New Zealand-based media monitoring agency. Some of our public relations clients use www.scoopit.co.nz for media measurement and evaluation purposes. Scoopit is a New Zealand community social bookmarking site."

STARS IN THEIR EYES

Delicious.com lets people bookmark a URL while others let people vote (sometimes down as well as up) for true crowd sourcing. This is the next step up the engagement food chain Ratings (Figure 5.1). How many stars did they give you?

Different services use different monikers, but the concept of using popularity to rank specific recourses is very popular (Table 5.1).

Star ratings are a very simple score to keep. If you keep your head above two-and-a-half out of five, then your focus is on beating your own score. But the ultimate goal is to get

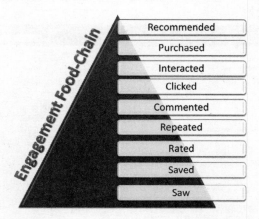

Figure 5.1 The Engagement Food Chain ranks the value of various engagements.

Table 5.1 There are lots of ways for people to note your efforts in a positive way.

Service/Site	Approbation
Digg	Digg
Facebook	Friend
Friendfeed	Likes
Reditt	Upvotes-Downvotes
Stumbleupon	I like this
Technorati	Favorite
Twitter	Favorite
Tumblr	Heart
Yahoo	Buzz Up

your story at the top of the news. Yahoo! Buzz has been letting people identify the most important/interesting stories for years (Figure 5.2).

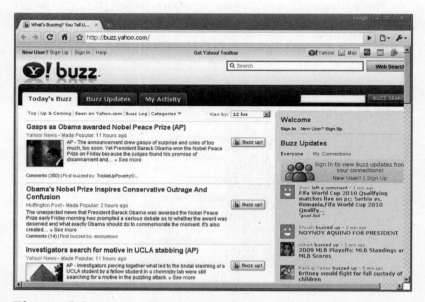

Figure 5.2 You can help lift a story to the top of the heap by giving it a Buzz Up on Yahoo!

TAG, YOU'RE IT

From there, it's time to put on your thinking cap and examine how people are tagging your links. Each time a resource is saved, the saver can add tags to it. A story about iPhones will definitely get tagged "iphone" but may also be tagged:

development

sdk (software development kit)

tutorial

design

hack

ringtone

reviews

aps

unlock

Jeremiah Owyang of Altimeter Group (www. altimetergroup.com) recommends keeping an eye on how the public categorizes their bookmarks of your links. "If you're a web strategist," Jeremiah says, "you should be looking inside of these tools, look up your content (and your competitor's content) and see how the content has been tagged, commented on, and what members have said ... Tie this into your web marketing efforts, the keywords that folks are tagging information with should also extend to your Search Engine Optimization programs such as metatagging your content, or making text match the same keywords. Also consider extending these keywords into the Search Engine

Marketing keywords that you'll be buying. After all, this is how the end user or consumer is thinking about your web page."

Repeating Revisited

Seeing, saving, rating, and tagging are all good, but repeating is much better. Previously covered, it's a placeholder and is included here as a reminder that there is a hierarchy of response.

From the perspective of *reach*, repeating your words to others is more valuable than writing a comment on your blog. But from the visitor's perspective, hitting a retweet button or copy-and-pasting your words is far easier and less self-revealing than composing their own opinion and posting for all to see.

Craving Comments

Avinash Kaushik (www.kaushik.net) is right on the money when he asks, "Are we having a conversation?" His is the measurement of whether people are engaged with your blog.

Measure how many comments you get and you'll know when you've touched a nerve. Review the types of posts that get the most comments and you'll not only be able to identify your most fervent fans and sharpest detractors, you'll be able to determine what sort of articles and opinions drive passions in your industry. This instant feedback can guide an author and inform the company.

In *Web Analytics 2.0*, Avinash offers up this definition of a Conversation Rate for measuring your blog:

*Conversation Rate answers the next question, "Are
we having a conversation?" It also helps you identify whether you are actually publishing content
that engages your audience.*

*Conversation Rate = # of Visitor comments/# of
posts.*

Avinash then discusses how much the author has contributed and how much the readers have commented—by
posts and comments and number of words. While useful, I
prefer to use the term "comments" as a purer number so as
to reserve "conversation" for later in an actual sales cycle.
Thus we see the difference between measuring a blog for
blog's sake versus a blog for business purposes.

Comments are a sincere form of commitment. When
you've struck a chord that resonates so well that others are
compelled to sing along, you will continue to attract people
to your brand. But there are other, more subtle indications
of engagement. Let's start with the inbound link.

Broadcasts Out of the Blue

Twitter, blogs, Facebook, Flickr—all places where people
can—and will—mention your company or your products
because you are on their mind. That may not be a direct
response to some action you've taken, but a response to all
the actions you have taken.

Among the For Sale tweets and the mentions of the
Kodak Theatre in Hollywood, Figure 5.3 shows that people
have Kodak on their minds.

They use their own measurement tools at Omniture
where Matt Langie keeps an eye on the online conversation.
They reach out to those social sites that have application

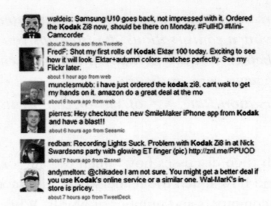

Figure 5.3 Somewhere, somebody at Kodak is—or should be—keeping a close eye on how people communicate about their brand sua sponte.

programming interfaces (API's) and pull the data back into Site Catalyst, their marketing metrics tool, to report on how many times the company or a product brand is mentioned.

"There are three major ways to look at it," says Matt. "One is in the context of reactivity. So, how do people react to your campaigns? How do they react to an email that you've sent out? How do they react to a product that you've announced? At Omniture, we look at tweets and mentions on a comparative or trended basis. When we do a really big announcement that seems to have captivated the industry (like the announcement that they were being purchased by Adobe) the numbers skyrocket."

Comparative measurement is critical as there are no industry benchmarks. If you have a socially active blogger or tweeter on staff, you're going to generate more buzz in the social media world. So comparing mentions and traffic against your own history is the only way to go for now.

"The second major area that we look at," Matt continues, "is productivity. This is where users are contributing content. So, someone watches a video on YouTube and posts a comment saying I love the video, I hate the video. Wasn't that silly. Wasn't that funny. What have you."

Click Happy

I started out in sales. The only reason for marketing was to get me in front of a prospective client. The lead was the thing, the only thing. Today, all the social media in the galaxy with all the lovely comments in the universe does nothing if it does not drive traffic to your web site, your telephone, or the store. I want clicks to my web site!

It's good that you have a way to see if there are storm clouds on the horizon, but what you really want to know is whether all this socializing is having an impact on the metrics that are components of my key business performance indicators. Let's try that again: Is it driving business?

Tracking the actions that result from all your blogging, tweeting, and YouTubing is where the money is. So we start at the very first reaction beyond talking about you even more—did they click? Or to quote Woody Allen, "Ninety percent of life is just showing up."

Avinash Kaushik coined "Average Shared Links Click-Through Rate" (CTR) which he admits is a tedious name, but it is accurate. Web visits might be the easiest thing to measure, given the plethora of marketing measurement tools from Omniture, Webtrends, and Coremetrics along with the free web analytics tools from Google and Yahoo!.

At the start, tracking a web site visitor back where they last were on the Web is straight forward. This one came from a Google search, that one from a press release, and the next from a banner ad. Social media is not as transparent and that's where coding your URLs is necessary and

Figure 5.4 Which shortened URLs are getting traffic and how much?

where sites like Bit.ly and Tr.im are crucial. Those, like Twitclicks, Tweetburner, and Clop.in shorten long URLs and then track the number of clicks they redirected on your behalf.

For example, there are two shortened URLs in Figure 5.4, one for a contest and one for a blog posting.

While the shortened URL in the tweet linking to the blog post got more direct clicks than the contest link, the contest link was spread around more. The 116 clicks that came from my tweet represent less than half of my traffic. This suggests there are significant differences between what's interesting and what's really interesting.

For messages you send out yourself, you can embed a tracking code in the URL. Add a question mark at the end of the link, followed by a unique code that identifies the campaign, and that code shows up in your web analytics reports. The link shorteners make it all the easier, as they will retain that code.

If you do not use a link shortener that includes metrics, traffic from tweeters who link to your site directly are likely to show up in your web analytics reports as either being from Twitter with no indication of who's tweeted, or they look like a "direct" visit where somebody typed in your domain name and page location directly.

You can track clicks to your web site back to the blogs that posted the links . . . unless they too have been using link shorteners. Then you'll need to hire a coder to help cobble together the variety of APIs and data streams. But what if the connection between the posted, hosted, or tweeted mention of your product was one step further removed? What if there were no link at all?

Problems like this are the food, wine, and dessert for small, agile technology companies. Tealium (www.tealium.com) has come up with an intriguing approach that can shed a lot of light. They scour the Web for mentions of your company and then tell you whether an individual visitor has seen your name mentioned elsewhere—even if that visitor did not click on that link at that time or there was no link.

In order words, Tealium can tell you if one mention of your company is enough to drive traffic or if a person needs to come across a mention of your firm several times before they finally click. In advertising, this is known as "view through." It's not limited to just brand names, either.

Here's how Tealium explains it:

Tealium's clients identify the keywords for which they want to monitor inclusions in news articles, blogs, as well as online video sites such as YouTube. Usually, the identified keywords are the company's name, web site address, ticker symbol, product or executive names. Once identified, the keywords will be used to retrieve clippings on the Internet, classified by news, blogs, video, etc. Upon visitors landing on the company's web site, the Tealium Social Media patent-pending technology will identify whether the visitor has been exposed to a specific social media content that has been indexed.

If you're in need of a report that proves to upper management that social media is driving traffic, this would be a good place to begin.

Is That Supposed to Be Funny?

Imitation may be the sincerest form of flattery, but satire is still flattery—although it may be insincere and far from flattering. Satire is a sign that you have become large enough to be a target.

Measure it, yes; control it, no. There are many stories, starting with the Coke/Mentos video, of companies that tried to shut down an embarrassing online conversation only to discover that it can't be done. The discovery is usually in public and quite embarrassing. Instead, embrace those having fun at your expense and encourage them. Make a contest of it.

In a blog post called "When will the world make fun of you?" Seth Godin says, "Spread the word, share the story. If it's worth telling, it's worth parodying. When will we be able to parody what you do?" (See http://sethgodin.typepad.com/seths_blog/2009/10/when-will-the-world-make-fun-of-you.html).

When parodies are not in good fun. When online comments are not accurate, then it's time to call the lawyers.

For an in-depth and thoughtful look at how to measure your YouTube exposure, take a look at a blog post from Peter Kowalski, director of research strategy at KDPaine & Partners called "How to Measure YouTube: Set up a simple measurement program, decide if particular videos are really problems, and prepare for the worst case scenario" (www.themeasurementstandard.com/issues/5-1-08/kowalskiyoutube5-1-08.asp). There's also a good review of the tool YouTube Insight by Jake Matthews at www.10e20.com/blog/2008/07/15/video-optimization-and- analytics-a-closer-look-at-youtube-insight/.

Post-Click Engagement

Once the clicker has arrived on your web site, an entirely different set of metrics kicks into place. The world of web analytics is constantly changing and has fascinated me for 10 years. I wrote a book called *Web Metrics: Proven Methods for Measuring Web Site Success* and founded the eMetrics Marketing Optimization Summit (www.emetrics.org) as well as the Web Analytics Association (www.WebAnalyticsAssociation.org)—yes, I am fascinated.

Interactivity after the click is your persuasion process at work. This is where your specific company goals meet a wide variety of tools to measure whether your marketing is on the money or missing the mark.

The Buy Now Button

While this may be the ultimate onsite/on-phone/in-the-store question, it is also applicable to social media. Yes, people are buying directly from blog posts and tweets.

Figure 5.5   Dell, ahead of the pack selling on the Internet, is now out in front selling via Twitter

Twitter.com/delloutlet (Figure 5.5) "sells certified, refurbished, scratch & dent and previously ordered new Dell products at great prices." What's not to love? They tweet great deals; you click and buy. From the budget conscious (that would be all of us from time to time) to the corporate buyer, this represents a way to get a quick check on something you planned to buy anyway or a chance to take advantage of a once-in-a-lifetime offer.

As of June 2009, Dell had hit the $3 million mark in sales, putting to rest any question of whether this constituted a new and valuable means of communication.

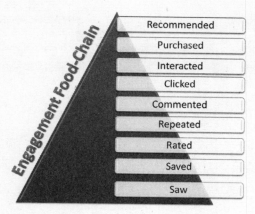

Figure 5.6   Engagement Food Chain

The final step up the engagement food chain (Figure 5.6) is recommendations. That's a great place to begin a look at how well your company is listening to the conversation out there. It's important enough to deserve its own chapter called Getting the Message—Hearing the Conversation.

CHAPTER 6

Getting the Message—Hearing the Conversation

Do you hear what I hear?

No, I'm not talking about the Christmas carol. I'm referring to the Voice of the Customer.

In the early 1980s (pre-PC), I was selling business computers to companies that had never had one before. The technology was new, the market was new, and smaller businesses didn't have a clue. I thought my sales manager was pressing the point about frugality by taking me to a local coffee shop for lunch and avoiding places with tablecloths and candles, but in fact, he was teaching me to tune my ears.

I learned more about how to sell computers by listening to the people at the tables around me than I ever did on sales calls, from company brochures, or from any amount of technical study. Computers were the talk of the town. It would be a few years before they made it to the cover of *Time* magazine as the "Man of the Year" and a dozen years before the Internet had that honor.

These business lunch eaters were concerned about things I was unprepared to explain. They were focused on business processes, organizational change, and staff

123

training. They were talking about placing their faith in something that heretofore was only useful for putting a man on the moon. These issues all had to be addressed before they'd trust a computer with their information and long before they'd trust a computer salesman who only talked about speeds, feeds, chips, and MIPS (millions of instructions per second). Listening to the voice of the customer allowed me to be a successful consultative salesman.

In their seminal book *The Cluetrain Manifesto* (www .cluetrain.com), those 1999 thought leaders laid down the law. "The marketplace is a conversation," they said. Companies can either join the conversation or go crazy trying to shout their message into it. The first sign of conversational incompatibility was the invention of the price tag in the late 1800s.

John Wanamaker is most noted for his comment "I know half my advertising is wasted, I just don't know which half." He also was the first to copyright an ad and the first to standardize pricing in his department store in Philadelphia, inventing the price tag. Before that, price was determined through haggling—a conversation.

So rather than thinking of social media as a new tool to push your message out there, and measuring the volume of your shrieking, rather than merely counting the number of ears your message invades, be aware that social media is much more powerful as a tool to help you converse. Every woman on the planet will tell every would-be boyfriend or spouse that conversation is a fine art and depends almost entirely on one's ability to listen. Customers will tell you the same thing ... if you'll only listen.

Listen to Them Search

Search has always been considered a regular part of regular online marketing and not a social media activity. From the advertiser's perspective, it's a great way to catch people who are interested at the moment. But what people are searching for—at the moment—represents public interests the same way tweets do.

♦ What are you doing?

♦ What are you thinking?

♦ What are you looking for?

These are all closely aligned questions and marketers are recognizing the value in analyzing the answers. When people arrive at your web site from a search engine, they are looking for something in particular and are communicating their intent. When they search for something *on* your web site (through your onsite search), they are communicating their inability to find it through your normal navigation menus. Both are instructive.

But more important in the realm of social media, how people discuss you Out There has a hefty impact on how many people will find their way to your web site (In Here) via search engines.

Crispin Sheraden is senior director of search marketing strategy and manages global search for SAP, an enterprise software company. That means they sell software and services for customer relationship management, enterprise resource planning, product lifecycle management, supply chain management, and a lot more.

Crispin's job is to support the regional hubs and their individual country operations. He immediately grasped the implications of social media to search. "At the start of 2008," he relates, "we realized halfway through our organic search project that we needed to influence social media to support our rankings. Nobody else was doing it so we jumped in headlong. And first thing we did was deploy the AddThis (www.addthis.com) functionality across pretty much every content page we have. It pops up all the Facebook, Twitter, Digg This, Reddit little check-it buttons."

Crispin tells it this way:

We started measuring and reporting out on the usage of that button. How many people were sharing or bookmarking content, and what kind of content they were sharing and bookmarking.

Everything else that we had seen before or shared before in terms of metrics around search was really focused on our very key top level pages. We found that deeper-level pages that focused on demos or even things that focused on community were getting the most sharing activity. Previously, it hadn't registered that there was so much interest in these deep, fairly shallowly-trafficked pages. There was some heat spots amongst those deeper pages that I think people were unaware of that we've now brought to life. So we have been able to focus the content organization on pages that would otherwise have been considered low-priority.

Content that gets less traffic but higher social sharing attention becomes the focus of keyword research and search marketing decisions. We can also give the content side of the house insight into how to fragment and build additional pages so that maybe a whole page on supply chain becomes a lot more about inventory management. Or we have the teams build some unique pages on inventory management alone. And those pages begin to rank more effectively and we begin to drive traffic.

Best of all, we found that those search-driven or social search-driven content pages we've recommended that have been built, are converting—capturing someone's email address and other contact information—three to four times the rate versus every other page on the site on average.

Crispin is focused on the practical side of selling specific software solutions to specific business problems. His goal is to drive more traffic that results in more qualified leads. Is that social media? It will be.

Search really will become a social endeavor now that startups are talking about making everything more social. Do a search and not only will you see what the search engine feels is the most relevant to your query, but it will show you what your friends have clicked on recently, having searched for something similar. If all your mother clicked on was a link after searching for "chicken stock," you can surmise her interests are culinary. If your father clicks on a link after searching for "chicken stock," you can guess he's wondering if he should sell his Tyson (TSN) holdings and buy more shares of Pilgrim's Pride (PGPDQ.PK).

Listen to Them Rate

We touched on ratings in Chapter 5 in the section called "Stars in Their Eyes." It bears repeating that a simple system set up to monitor fluctuations in ratings across multiple ratings sites can prove useful.

We're not looking for absolute scores here, just directional information that gives you a clue when something happens. If your scores suddenly skyrocket, you should be aware. Should they plummet, you should be very aware.

Listen to Them Praise

It's ecstasy when a customer unexpectedly tweets or posts something nice about you. It feels wonderful. People you have never met, showing you the love. But as self-serving, ego-inflating, and crass as it may seem, measuring the love is an important part of your job.

If 200 people sing your praises every day, it makes you feel great. Should you take it amiss if only 100 sing your praises tomorrow? Yes. Does it mean your company is doing something wrong? Not necessarily, but it can mean you're not doing things as right as you were and that's worth noting.

They're not unhappy—they're just not going on about it. Why not? Perhaps they were thrilled with your product or service on day one and then they got used to having whiter whites and brighter colors from your daily washday miracle. Maybe the coolness factor of your new phone was replaced with a warm glow of satisfaction that no longer needed to be boasted about in public. That's all very logical when looking at the individual, but the individual is not the important player here; the marketplace is—an aggregate of individuals.

The actual numbers here are not as important as the percent change—always keep an eye on the trend line. If hundreds praise you every day, then that's the baseline against which you want to gauge how much contentment you are spreading in the world. If that trend reverses, it's time to read each one and find out if there's a shift in praise-worthiness.

You get new customers every day. Every day there are people being overwhelmed by the taste of your secret sauce for the first time, astonished at the speed of your laptop for the first time, or impressed by how your plumber showed up right on time to install the dishwasher.

If the number of unbridled exclamations of approval drops over time, then the entire marketplace is changing. Your product is still great, but it's just not engaging the hearts and minds of your customers the way it used to. Call it customer expectation inflation. Call your customers jaded. But listen carefully for when the buzz about your products start to fade. It's a sign.

There are also signals hidden inside their praise. If your proponents are advocating your firm more for "great prices" than "outstanding products" or "terrific service" then you may have a problem. If the quantity of adoration stays the same but the subject shifts from "couldn't live without" to "really funny pictures on their web site" or "I hope I win the trip to Tahiti," then you have a problem that needs prompt attention.

If you sell goods and service to the masses, there may be an easier way to read what's on customers' minds—the published review. Published reviews are so popular that they have engendered an industry.

Listen to Them Review

Many studies have been done (Econsultancy, eMarketer, JupiterResearch, Marketing Profs, etc.) reaching the same conclusion: People have more faith in peers than in advertisers. No surprise there whatsoever. A used car salesman in a loud plaid sport coat is nowhere near as plausible as a total stranger at a football game. (Warning: That stranger at the game may be an off-duty used car salesman in disguise!)

BAD REVIEWS ARE YOUR FRIEND

Every marketer knows that testimonials reassure prospective customers and it follows that user-generated reviews would be enticing as well. Naturally, this makes marketers fearful. If you allow random customers to comment on your products, they might say something bad about you. Can't have that. Must manage the message. Must control the brand image.

As this book is about social media, you know the admonition that follows such statements: "You can't control the conversation anyway so stop trying." I don't presume to be quite so naive. You can't control the conversation but you can guide the conversation. You can influence the conversation. You can have an impact on the conversation. That's the whole reason for tracking and measuring it.

But do not for a moment think that you can keep the conversation all happiness and light. In fact, you do not want everybody saying nice things about you and your goods and services. Really.

All those previously mentioned studies have also shown that a single negative review dramatically raises the credibility of all the other, positive reviews. Ten excellent reviews make people feel a little better but nine good reviews plus one bad one that bashes the product will noticeably increase sales.

Case in point: I was about to buy my fourth Sony Vaio laptop but wanted to be sure there were no gotchas. I didn't want to buy blind. So off I went to the reviews and found many others who were very happy with the specific laptop I wanted to buy. Among the commendations, none of which were of interest, were a fair number of negative evaluations that fell into three categories. Two people complained that the keyboard stopped functioning when they doused, drenched, or drizzled the poor things with water, coffee, or soft drinks. I had no plans to use my laptop underwater, undercoffee, or undermountaindew.

The next was a common complaint. The machines came with way too much software and the simple task of removing programs from the Control Panel has removed lots of other bits and pieces that have caused most of the rest of the programs to cease functioning. I've been on the planet long enough to have done that . . . but only once.

The third one had to do with the buyer getting a machine with an insufficient amount of random access memory. I've done that as well . . . twice.

So by the time I had read a few dozen reviews, I was convinced that I should buy my adored Sony Vaio laptop as long as I was prepared to protect it from the effects of water on microscopic electronic components and was careful with the bloatware that passes as code these days. If these were the worst things people had to say, I had nothing to worry about.

If the product managers at Sony were reading the same reviews I was, all they learned was that they could recommend more memory and maybe make their keyboards waterproof. The former was a pricing issue and the latter might help a small segment of their customers. But if they listen carefully and listen well, they can learn a great deal about what their next product offering might look like.

SYNDICATED REVIEWS BUILD SALES

The fact that customer reviews increase sales was the motive for a company called Bazaarvoice, founded by a man who had previously founded a web analytics company (Bret Hurt, Coremetrics) and another who used to do web analytics for one of the world's largest computer sellers (Sam Decker, Dell).

Bazaarvoice offers software and services to syndicate customer reviews of products across scores of web sites. If you're selling a certain model of luggage that can be found on a hundred web sites, you can display reviews posted on all of those sites provided that they too are Bazaarvoice customers.

The measurements prove that sales web sites with reviews perform much better than those without. In the early fall of 2008, online plumbing retailer Vintage Tub & Bath was enjoying an increase in sales of more than 12.5 percent while their main competitors were going up at nearly 28 percent. By September, Vintage was working with Bazaarvoice and had over 1,000 reviews on their site. Then the stock market dropped like a stone and the purchase of high-end bathroom fixtures hit the floor. In September, Vintage's sales dropped almost 9 percent. However, one of their competitor's businesses declined by nearly 30 percent in the same time period.

Bad Reviews Improve Products

By keeping an eye on syndicated reviews, children's furniture seller The Land of Nod discovered how to make product improvements.

One of their products was a play/activity table for kids. It scored 4.8 out of 5 stars. People liked it a lot and 90 percent gave it that all-powerful "would recommend it to a friend" accolade. But a closer review of the reviews revealed that customers felt the surface of the table was too prone to scratching.

The product designers discovered a harder type of wood that was more scratch-resistant and offered a new version of the table. The marketing team reached out to those who had mentioned this product inadequacy; they offered a replacement to those who had spoken out. Customer service became great customer service, happy customers became advocates, and everybody who buys from The Land of Nod knows they are dealing with a company that knows how to listen.

Random reviews are valuable for product development (they tell you what they want) and for product marketing (they tell you what resonates). It can also be the best promotional material ever. When your customers tell the world that your product rocks, it's the best possible advertisement—and some would say the single most important metric ever.

You always hope to overhear: "Oh, I've been using Brand X for years and it's the best thing since sliced bread—even better!" That's more than a mention. It's more than a compliment. It's more than a willingness to wear your T-shirt or sport your logo on their backpack. It's somebody putting their personal reputation on the line by telling others that you are worthy. It's very nice, but is it important? Some say it's the only meaningful metric out there.

Listen to Them Recommend

The Net Promoter Score asks one, ultimately important question: "Are you likely to recommend our company to a friend or colleague?" This, according to developer Frederick Reichheld, is the best single question you can ask a customer to find out how loyal they are. "The net of promoters minus detractors doesn't show up in profit and loss statements," Frederick says, "but detractors destroy your future."

Tektronix finds surprising results from Net Promoter Scores

The issue over which marketing benchmarks to use has become a simple one for Martyn Etherington, VP of marketing at Tektronix, a Portland, Ore.-based manufacturer of test and measurement equipment.

As a market leader, Tektronix didn't see a lot of upside in many of the activities and metrics that track customer acquisition. Rather, its goal became figuring out where growth could come from the business it already had.

The company certainly was motivated. Like many others, Tektronix suffered in the 1990s after a period of diversification followed by consolidation and retrenchment. But the company survived the high-tech bust and emerged looking for growth that was more organic and solid.

To that end, Etherington in 2006 began to focus on one decidedly low-tech metric he became convinced could help Tektronix grow: analyzing customer loyalty as indicated by their Net Promoter Score. The score, a concept developed by customer loyalty expert Fred Reichheld and popularized by his book *The Ultimate Question*, suggests a business can gauge its customers' loyalty—and, significantly, their potential business—by asking the question "How likely is it that you would recommend us to a friend or colleague?"

"What we found was, some of our customers whom we thought we had absolute water-tight relations with, the Net Promoter Score indicated otherwise," Etherington said. "In other cases, it went off the scale."

Working with Laura Patterson, president of VisionEdge Marketing, Etherington surveyed Tektronix's top 40 accounts, subtracting the percentage of "detractors" from promoters to get an overall NPS number. The company also focused closely on the NPS results of individual customers.

A SIMPLE QUESTIONNAIRE

Etherington's main tool was a simple questionnaire, probing with other questions (besides the ultimate one) underlying reasons for particular responses; follow-up phone conversations delved deeper.

Today, the process has been institutionalized at Tektronix. The ultimate question is asked of certain visitors to the company's web site, after technical support tasks are completed and following sales closings. NPS numbers are reviewed monthly within Tektronix's four global regions, and deeper studies are conducted each quarter. A simple nod to automation is in the form of dashboards, which track the NPS results.

(continued)

(continued)

"Everything green is great, and things that are red we jump on with phone calls and counter measures," Etherington said. "Actually, the discipline and accountability are primary, the tool is secondary. I'm happy with spreadsheets and duct tape—anything that can give us answers."

Since NPS results didn't quite square with internal expectations, Etherington said, there was some skepticism and defensiveness, in particular from salespeople who sometimes viewed low NPS results as direct criticisms of their own job performance.

"But that wasn't where we wanted to go," he said. "We wanted to make sure this never was meant to be punitive, but rather as indicators for future growth."

Now that its largely manual measurement phase is complete, the company has begun work with customer experience management firm Satmetrix to implement a more automated process to track exactly where performance can be improved and detail the complexities of its customers' propensity to provide more sales in every area of their own operations.

"We have shown above-market growth over the past two years in those customers that have higher Net Promoter Scores," Etherington said. "And we're working to get more of the average scores to move right, to find where the problems lie. As for the very lowest, those customers just may not be good fits for us."

Originally published in B-to-B Online (www.btobonline.com) June 9, 2008. Reproduced with permission from VisionEdge Marketing.

"Would you recommend?" is an interesting question to ask, but there's debate about whether it is really indicative of future performance. Yes, I'd recommend my real estate agent, but I've lived in the same house for 20 years and have no plans to move. Yes, I'd recommend my dentist but have no plans to consume more of his services. You have to get into the details to know how and where to leverage customer attitude to improve your business.

Survey companies like iPerceptions (www.iperceptions .com) and OpinionLab (www.opinionlab.com) are great for spotting specific problem areas and tracking the shift in opinion as changes are made to a product, a web site, or a company.

Another benchmark of hearts and minds can be found at ForeSee Results (www.foreseeresults.com) (Figure 6.1). While there are many survey tools and services online, ForeSee Results stands out for its use of the American Customer Satisfaction Index (ACSI) (www.theacsi.org) model, which links customer expectations, perceived

Figure 6.1 ForeSee Results has tied customer satisfaction survey results to financial performance.

quality, and perceived value to customer satisfaction through a set of causal equations. ACSI tracks trends in customer satisfaction through a rigid methodology that is, therefore, highly comparable. It's a national economic indicator of satisfaction with goods and services.

ForeSee Results brings two interesting components to the table. First, they have shown that the index they use is a predicator of a company's financial performance—improving satisfaction scores predict improving stock value and therefore price. Second, they identify which specific things are drivers of satisfaction whether it be price, web site content, or call center resolution speed. Customers might say price is critical, but it may not impact satisfaction as much as a better search capability on the company web site.

Keep in mind that we've been discussing surveys. Surveys let you know what customers are willing to tell you. I strongly recommend continuing the direct conversation with your customers. They will tell you things about your products and services that are simply not interesting to their friends and followers. They will tell you where you are going wrong. Nevertheless, let's stay focused on the social side—what they say to each other.

The simplest tracking method (and free) has to be the Google Alert. Just set up a search for "I would recommend (your product/company)." As with all sentiment analysis, it's easy enough to watch for "I would *not* recommend . . ." but this is tricky when humans get playful.

I recommend Mammoth Hide Tissues for anybody with a nose as soft as a camel's.

I recommend the latest *Rocky* movie if you stop for a lobotomy on the way to the theater.

I recommend Hummers for those who are brainless about the environment.

Although listening isn't simple, it is useful.

As an advertising-supported web site, the *Washington Post* cares about page views, and Rochelle Sanchirico, senior director of acquisition marketing, monitors the traffic that Facebook and Twitter drive to their site. She tracks the value of that traffic not just by the number of pages, but which ones. "Some pages are more valuable to us," Rochelle says, "because they are targeted to a more specific reader and advertisers will pay more for those types."

But the *Washington Post* is also interested in what people are saying about them, their web site, and the content of their articles. At a Web managers' roundtable in Washington, D.C., in the fall of 2009, Rochelle was asked about the tools they use to decipher attitude and find recommendations. "Interns" was her reply. Yes, it sometimes simply takes a human.

Listen to Them Complain

Complaints come in many shapes and sizes. Generic complaints are there to be counted, but specific complaints are there to be gratefully received. If they are complaining about a specific product feature or service error, you can gauge how many people feel the same way and whether their attitude is shifting over time.

FOCUSED GRIEVANCES

The primary reason for listening to complaints is the social networking nature of social networking. If somebody is unhappy with you for some reason and they are creative in their criticism, you may be on the receiving end of a severe and very public tongue-lashing.

Remember the YouTube hit *United Breaks Guitars*? Here's the short version of the story by songwriter Dave Carroll:

> *In the spring of 2008, Sons of Maxwell were travel-*
> *ing to Nebraska for a one-week tour and my Taylor*
> *guitar was witnessed being thrown by United Air-*
> *lines baggage handlers in Chicago. I discovered*
> *later that the $3,500 guitar was severely damaged.*
> *They didn't deny the experience occurred but for*
> *nine months the various people I communicated*
> *with put the responsibility for dealing with the*
> *damage on everyone other than themselves and*
> *finally said they would do nothing to compensate*
> *me for my loss. So I promised the last person to*
> *finally say "no" to compensation (Ms. Irlweg) that*
> *I would write and produce three songs about my*
> *experience with United Airlines and make videos*
> *for each to be viewed online by anyone in the*
> *world. (www.davecarrollmusic.com/story/united-*
> *breaks-guitars)*

He did. The result? A YouTube hit (www.youtube .com/watch?v=5YGc4zOqozo) (See Figure 6.2.).

From a pure public relations perspective, keeping an ear open is fundamental. But the value of monitoring com-plaints goes beyond just staying tuned for surprises.

TOPIC TRENDING

Opinion about whether your software is secure enough, your wastewater is clean enough, or your prices competitive

Figure 6.2   More than half a million people will think twice about flying United.

enough will change over time. Tracking and trending on complaints gives your company real insight into prioritizing what needs to be addressed.

Assume for a minute that you work for a car company. In an oversimplified example, Figure 6.3 shows the trends in conversation over time. Clearly, environmental issues are the biggest trending topic when it comes to automobiles or a particular brand or a particular 0078 model.

TANTRUM TWEETING

Your company may have already worked through this moment in its history or you may be facing the prospect of customers screaming bloody murder about you—in public. They're not shouting on blogs or opinion forums but out into tweet-space.

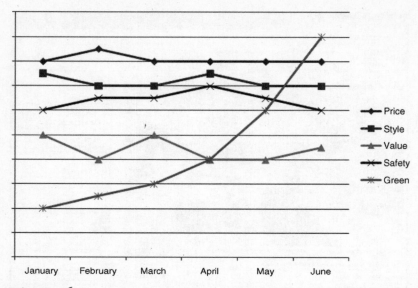

January February March April May June

◆	Price
■	Style
▲	Value
✕	Safety
✳	Green

Figure 6.3   A strong signal to car companies that the environment has the public's attention at the moment and is trending higher.

For examples of frustrated people taking their lack of anger management to Tweetsville, the easiest target is mobile phone service:

- ◆ Aeroplan + their gross inflexibility = terrible customer service.

- ◆ It took an hour of fiddling with the modem and 30 minutes of mindless jabber with Verizon.

- ◆ Wow, AT&T really is garbage in NYC. I've had more dropped calls in one day than in three years in Toronto!

Not everybody agrees on which is worse:

- ◆ OMG no matter how bad you say AT&T is, Cricket Wireless is.

♦ 1000x WORSE! Spent an hour on the phone and can't even get a person! #servicefail.

Seems like a good idea to set up a Twitter search for your company name and the hashtag "#ServiceFail."

But when an entire new hashtag is created just for your organization, along with a specific Twitter account *and* an icon made up of your logo with a slash line through it, you know you have a customer satisfaction problem (Figure 6.4).

My reference to "this moment in history" is based on the premise that Twitter offers a terrific metric indicating that your customer service is below tolerable. If people have to complain into the masses via their keyboard, the problem is big enough for you to take some serious action.

There will always be people disparaging your goods and services—especially if you're selling cell phone service. But the recency and frequency of complaints should be on your

Figure 6.4 Vodafone customers are uniting in their displeasure.

mind or at least on your dashboard so you can monitor when people are "taking it to the streets."

Ask Them to Participate

The basic premise of social media is that it is Out There and you can't control it. In fact, you shouldn't try to control it. But you can bring it in closer. You can bring the social aspect onto your premises (your web site) and encourage people to be a part of a subject-specific conversation—that subject being your goods and services.

> You know better than anyone else what you want from Starbucks. So tell us. What's your Starbucks Idea? Revolutionary or simple—we want to hear it. Share your ideas, tell us what you think of other people's ideas and join the discussion. We're here, and we're ready to make ideas happen. Let's get started. (http://mystarbucksidea.force.com/)

It's a simple idea: Crowdsource ideas. Ask your customers to tell you how to make your service better. Then ask them to comment on those suggestions. Then ask them to vote on their suggestions. The most popular idea for Starbucks from customers? A bigger pat on the back to their workers (Figure 6.5).

This concept caught on big with computer manufacturer and seller Dell, which launched the IdeaStorm (www.ideastorm.com) in February 2007 (Figure 6.6).

From concept to implementation took all of three weeks. They were serious about knowing what their customers are thinking. That kind of movement at a company this size implies approval from the very top.

Figure 6.5 Starbucks customers want a closer relationship with their servers (Baristas). What could be better?

Figure 6.6 Dell's IdeaStorm was an instant success in the eyes of their customers.

"That implies it was Michael Dell's idea," says Vida Killian, Dell Idea Storm manager. "Michael heard about the idea from Mark Benioff, CEO at salesforce.com. And Michael wanted an easy way for anyone in the world to give us their ideas and a way to prioritize them. When Michael said he wanted it, we said sure, we'll give it to you in a few months. And he said how about in about three weeks, and there you go. So, we launched it very quickly, and we were hit with something like 2,000 ideas in the first two weeks."

There was no marketing behind it. They ran a beta version for a few weeks with a very closed audience and then Michael Dell announced it at a conference. Word got out fast. These days, Idea Storm enjoys a steady state of better than 400 ideas a week. Customers are thrilled that Dell is listening, and Dell is delighted to be on the receiving end of product improvement suggestions and the rest of their patrons voting on those ideas. Those are the easy metrics (Figure 6.7).

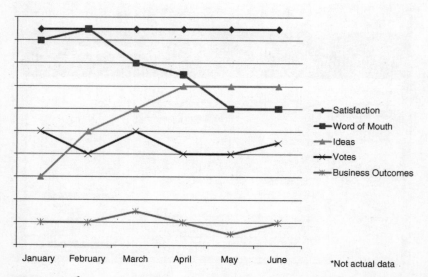

Figure 6.7 Everything looks good at IdeaStorm—except where the rubber meets the road.

Vida loves the reaction from customers but is a little hesitant about the reaction inside the company. "It's not a hundred percent success," says Vida and then she qualifies that quickly. "We have areas of the business that are welcoming of it with open arms. They're active, they're taking the feedback, they're using it on a regular basis. There are areas of the business that are interested in it if I help them find the relevant information because it is simply overwhelming to find the right idea to match the right part of the business.

"However, I have some portions of the business—a minority—that are not as interested because they don't know all of the specifics. They don't know what segment a given idea is coming from. They worry about the target audience. So, we focus on the areas of the business that are more engaged."

Vida monitors the categories on IdeaStorm. She makes sure the proper ideas filter into Popular, Recent, and Top ideas. Some of the most popular ideas are going nowhere. Everybody likes the idea of a standard power cable for laptops but implementation is all but impossible. Power supplies are unique to the device; plugs are not standardized around the world nor is the voltage of the power itself. But it's still a very powerful idea.

"If we have some coming in that are easy to jump on," Vida enthuses, "that we know we already offer it or it's on the road map or it's of interest to a different group, I'll filter those ideas to the right area.

"The real trick seems to be getting the right ideas and the proper details about who proposed the idea and what sort of customers are voting it up or down. As far as creating a culture and an environment within the company, I work with the product teams to understand their product development cycle. What is the best time for them to get the ideas? Then we set up reporting so it's not necessary for them to be on the site itself every day or every week."

Vida has a lot to keep track of—inside the company. She needs to know when and how to fertilize product managers' imaginations. If they have a new product release going out in a week, it might be better to hold off on sending them new ideas as they come in. "Right *after* a product release, very conveniently, it's the best time to look for ideas.

"For example, we had a complete upgrade from the D series to the E series of our Latitude machine. That team was very engaged on Idea Storm and implemented six very key features into the product. Right after a large announcement, we received ideas indicating people liked the new E series, but they wanted more—of course. But the product team was in the product planning cycle, moving on to the next product and very ready to hear new ideas. They were ready for the feedback."

Vida has her eyes on other metrics besides the number of ideas and votes. "We monitor the traffic in the sense of number of registered users, number of ideas, number of votes, number of comments. Your basic traffic numbers; we're watching that.

"I've also done some analysis recently on my top users because I get to know them. I mean, it's very obvious who's around all the time. Of 82,000 comments that we have right now, 80 percent come from 450 people. So back to your basic community one percent rule."

A really good idea that is very popular—and possible—is something no company can afford to shy away from. "About eleven percent of the ideas on the site are related to Linux." Vida says. "We were hit with 2,000 appeals for Linux in the first two weeks and we offered Linux within three months. The Linux community is very vibrant and two members of our Linux development team are constantly active on the site, responding to questions about when we'll release bios drivers and updates or offer these products in Europe and other parts of the world."

When it comes to other metrics, Vida has her eye on how many people look at but don't comment on ideas, how often people do or do not come back, which people are the most common commenters, etc. But she keeps her eyes open in other directions, too. "We do surveys, and we do focus groups. I want Idea Storm to be a part of that process and not the only input we count on."

In 2010, the plan is to link an individual's Idea Storm identity to his Dell.com profile provided he's given permission. This will give Dell a look at who this anonymous idea person is and then match him up with his onsite behavior. Suddenly, behavioral segmentation gets much more detailed. We know who the creative people are and we can see how they behave on the regular Dell web site.

Does Dell consider Idea Storm a success? Yes. They are looking at implementing private versions for large customers and have already implemented an internal version called Employee Storm. Think of it as the giant Suggest Box on the Intranet. They get half as many ideas as they do from their customers but considering the huge ratio between the two, that represents a huge level of internal interest.

So far, the external Idea Storm is holding its own with thousands of ideas, hundreds of thousands of votes, tens of thousands of comments, and hundreds of ideas implemented (Figure 6.8).

According to Vida, it just feels right. "I'm not a golfer but the few times that I've done it, when you hit that golf ball right you get excited because it actually goes somewhere! When I have an idea that's really hot and I find it's the right

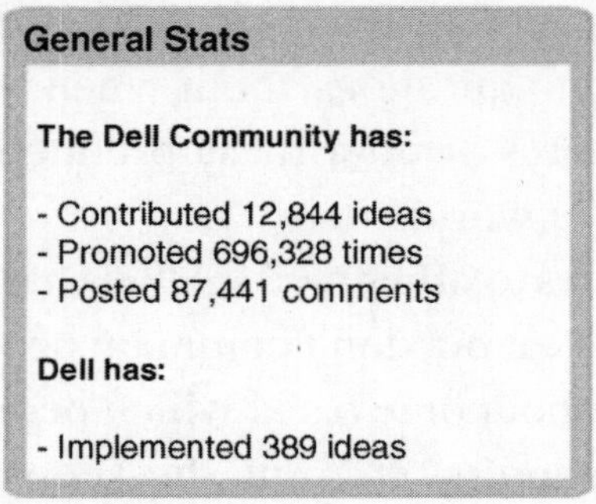

General Stats

The Dell Community has:

- Contributed 12,844 ideas
- Promoted 696,328 times
- Posted 87,441 comments

Dell has:

- Implemented 389 ideas

Figure 6.8 Dell's Idea Storm's numbers seem to speak for themselves.

person, and I get it to them at the right time, I see magic happen."

Magic is a metric we can all relate to.

Ask Them to Contribute

The truly transparent organization allows its customers to become part of their product design and development process. It starts with focus groups and surveys and ends up with advisory councils and partnership teams. The next step is inviting people to be part of the customer service team.

Some companies have tracked the number of customers who post to forums and kept track of who is the most helpful in answering others' questions.

Motorola was one of the first to create a wiki where customers could post their own "user manual." For their Q mobile phone, they had the usual list of online customer support options such as the Quick Start Guide, the (PDF) product manual, and the FAQs. Customers had all the formal instructions on using the phone. But Motorola said that didn't go far enough.

"Because the possible applications for the MOTO Q will always expand," Motorola said, "the 'ideal' user guide would also be able to grow and change. This wiki is an attempt to do that. It's a place to capture and share the knowledge of the greater community of MOTO Q users. If, for example, you have added a new application to your MOTO Q, you could post instructions on how you did it here, for the benefit of all MOTO Q users."

Allow your customers to help your customers. Often, they know more about your offerings than you do.

Listen, Listen, Listen—and Then Respond

Now that you've tuned your ears well enough to make neighborhood dogs and cave-dwelling bats jealous, it's time to be responsive.

Dell's Dell Outlet Twitter efforts are bolstered by the fact that they are managing customer service there as well (Figure 6.9).

How do you measure Twitter success? Eric T. Peterson interviewed Ben Grimes on the Web Analytics Demystified blog to find out. Ben is a customer service and support representative at marketing optimization provider Omniture. He realized Twitter was important, registered as @OmnitureCare, and immediately started fielding those questions that were asked of friends and followers.

When Eric asked, "What are your measures of success as a Twitter support rep?" Ben responded, "Certainly time to response and time to resolution are KPIs (Key Performance Indicators), but that goes without saying in customer support and relationship management. At this point, I suppose my goal is to leave 100 percent of clients who interact with me feeling more confident in their Omniture abilities.

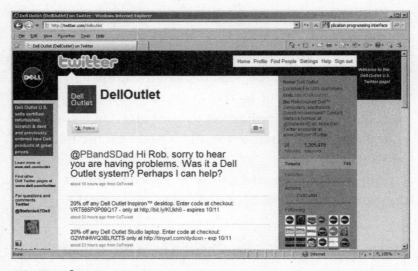

Figure 6.9   Dell sells on Twitter but listens and responds to customer comments and complaints as well.

It's always a success when I'm able to disseminate knowledge and help our customers get better value out of our tools."

Ben is right on the money. But what about metrics for a company with millions of customers and thousands of support people?

TWEETING CUSTOMER SERVICE

Recognizing the possibilities, Best Buy created an online suggestion box like Starbucks and Dell but they also created a sensation when they turned their Twitter channel over to all of their employees. The big splash was when they aired a series of TV commercials featuring lone customers in the middle of a stadium, addressing thousands of Best Buy service representatives in the stands (Figure 6.10).

Figure 6.10 This Best Buy TV ad was the first time many had ever heard of Twitter.

"Twelpforce" is an initiative that allows company employees to jump on to Twitter and answer whatever questions come along. It's like having everybody jump on the switchboard and answer random calls, but you can see which questions you'd like to answer.

John Bernier is a social media manager at Best Buy. "A" manager, as in one of many. How many? "Within our organization, the journey to social has been fairly organic," says John. "There isn't an organizational hierarchy that says, 'We have a senior director of social, and then we have two directors, each of whom oversee eight different social initiatives.' It's more collaborative and organic than that.

"Our Employee Customer Care Group created the Best Buy forums last year, and they work with our legal team to develop our publicly posted blogging and social media guidelines (http://bbyconnect.appspot.com/ participation_guidelines/). These are kind of lane bumpers with a compass north. We lay out for our employees who may not realize the significance of a presence that they create and maintain online. If you're an employee who works in the store, we want to just call out the fact that when you tell people you work for Best Buy, you are now placing a portion of the brand's reputation in your hands.

"The guidelines are not too constrictive because there is more than one way to meet and exceed customer expectations. There are going to be unique and innovated ways people can deliver something exceptional."

So what metrics do you use to determine the value of such a program?

John admits that there are a lot of things they would like to measure but simply can't yet. How does Twelpforce compare with Dell Outlet? How is positive word-of-mouth impacting store traffic nationally? Is this communication tool delivering on the brand promise of helpfulness?

For now, the Best Buy team is tracking brand value:

♦ Has Twelpforce positively or negatively impacted your impression of Best Buy?

♦ Has Twelpforce improved your perception of Best Buy's 24/7 availability?

♦ Has Twelpforce improved your perception of Best Buy's offering expert advice?

♦ Has Twelpforce improved your perception of Best Buy's ability to fix a problem?

♦ Did Twelpforce initiate a visit to a Best Buy store?

Is there hope for Twitter metrics to a sales and customer service organization? John says yes. "I think that will come because I recognized the gap. Others recognized the gap, and there are people who are going to build a business around it."

John is looking forward to following seasonal sales, call center contact reduction, and any shift in the types of issues people prefer to tweet about versus call about. Until then, you can hear the smile in his voice when he says, "As a group, we've answered over 8,000 questions in nearly eight weeks." Then you can hear the big, wide grin when he says, "We're changing the perception of Best Buy as a big giant yellow tag on the front of a blue building to one that is represented by 150,000 faces every day in this digital space."

RESPONDING TO A TWEDICAMENT

Can you measure the goodwill generated when the press and the bloggers and the tweeters all share the story about how you solved a problem that came your way via Twitter? Sure you can.

Just ask Virgin America. In-flight tweets prompted a representative to be at the landing gate with "customer recovery" coupons.

Ask StubHub, who got mentioned in the *New York Times* for noticing "a sudden surge of negative blog sentiment after rain delayed a Yankees-Red Sox game. Stadium officials mistakenly told hundreds of fans that the game had been canceled, and StubHub denied fans' requests for refunds, on the grounds that the game had actually been played. But after spotting trouble brewing online, the company offered discounts and credits to the affected fans. It is now re-evaluating its bad weather policy. 'This is a canary in a coal mine for us,' said John Whelan, StubHub's director of customer service." (www.nytimes.com/2009/08/24/technology/internet/24emotion.html)

Hearing Aids

I try to avoid getting deep into specific tools in my books. They change so fast that enumerating specific systems or services ends up more confusing than not over time. I'll leave that to those who do it for a living like Forrester Research and Gartner Research and those who do it for a passion like the thousands of bloggers who follow a wide variety of such things.

From newcomers like Teragram Sentiment Analysis Manager (www.teragram.com/solutions/sentiment-analysis.html), which scrapes reviews from Amazon and Overstock along with blogs and tweets to monitor how well products are rated by the masses, to time-honored firms like Nielsen with their BuzzMetrics service (http://en-us.nielsen.com/tab/product_families/nielsen_buzzmetrics), each has its own special something it brings to the party.

How Good a Listener Are You?

Social media strategist Jeremiah Owyang spelled out a social media listening maturity model in his November 10th, 2009 blogpost (www.web-strategist.com/blog/2009/11/10/evolution-the-eight-stages-of-listening/).

Web Strategy Matrix: The Eight Stages Of Listening

Stage	Description	Resources Needed	Impacts
1) No objective at all	Organization has a listening program but has no goals, nor uses the information for anything resourceful	Simple alerting tools, like Google Alerts and feedreaders will suffice.	At the basic level, simple self-awareness. Yet without any action from the data, this is useless.
2) Tracking of brand mentions	Like traditional "clip reports" of media relations, companies now track mentions in the social space. Despite tracking there is no guidance on what to do next.	Listening platform with report capability based on brand or product keywords. Radian 6, Visible Technologies, Techrigy/Alterian, Buzzmetrics and Cymfony, Dow Jones are providers.	Improved self-awareness to track volume of information, yet unable to track depth, and tonality of conversations. As a result, not a full understanding of opportunities.
3) Identifying market risks and opportunities	This proactive process involves seeking out discussions online that may result in identifying flare-ups, or possible prospect opportunities.	In addition to a listening platform staff must actively seek out discussions and signal to internal teams. Alerting tools, and listening platforms are required.	Organization can reduce risk of flare-ups before they become mainstream, identify prospects, and poach unhappy competitors customers.

(continued)

(*Continued*)

Stage	Description	Resources Needed	Impacts
4) Improving campaign efficiency	Rather than just measure a marketing effort after it's occurred, using tools to gauge during in-flight behavior yields real-time marketing efficiency.	Dedicated resource to manage reactions, activity, and sentiment to a marketing effort, and the resources to make course corrections nearly real-time. Traditional web analytics tools like Omniture, Webtrends, and Google Analytics are common.	Campaigns can be more effective, as hot spots are bolstered, and dead spots are diminished.
5) Measuring customer satisfaction	In addition to customer satisfaction scores, organizations can measure real-time sentiment as customers interact. Sysomos and Backtype have focus areas into this space.	Customer experience professionals will have to extend their scope to the social web, using a listening platform and sentiment analysis. Insight platforms like Communispace and Passenger offer online focus groups solutions.	Brands can now measure impacts of real time satisfaction or frustration during the actual phases of customer interaction. Then identify areas of improvement during customer lifecycle

6) Responding to customer inquiry	This proactive response finds customers where they are (fish where fish are) in order to answer questions. Example: Comcastcares account on Twitter asks customers if they need help—then may respond.	An active customer advocacy team that's empowered, training, and ready to make real-time responses nearly around the clock.	Customers will feel a greater sense of satisfaction, yet this teaches customers to 'yell in public' to get a response.
7) Better understand customers	Evolving the classic market research function, brands can improve their customer profiles and personas by adding social information to them.	Social CRM systems are quickly emerging that tie together a customer record and their online behavior, locations, and preferences. Salesforce, SAP, both have partnerships with Twitter to synch data	The opportunity to not only serve customers in their natural mediums, but to offer them a richer experience regardless of their customer touchpoints.

(continued)

(*Continued*)

Stage	Description	Resources Needed	Impacts
8. Being proactive and anticipating customers	Minority Report: This most sophisticated form actually anticipates what customers will say or do before they've done it. By looking at previous patterns of historical data, companies can put in place the right resources to guide prospects and customers.	An advanced customer database, with a predictive application put in place, as well as a proactive team to reach out to customers before an incident has happened. Haven't seen any such application yet.	Identifying prospects and engaging them before competitors can yield a larger marketing funnel, or reducing customer frustration as problems are fixed before they happen.

Professional Listening

A little bird told me—on the phone, not Twitter—that Procter & Gamble is getting serious about listening. He or she started his or her description to me with "You didn't hear it from me . . . but they're focusing on building out a listening service, aggregating, creating listening polls across the organization, disseminating information to the brands that needed it at the level they needed it and so on, and they're viewing this as an enterprise problem because they think it's going to transform for market research."

As well they should. Especially considering that they are a company that isn't just a business traveler's hotel chain or an airline with a somewhat narrow focus. When your target market, your audience, is everybody who might use toothpaste, that would be everybody. So you listen as hard as you can.

It used to be that the sacred word from the customer came from the sales department or the market research center. The sales reps would come back to headquarters and say, "I was talking to a customer and he said he wouldn't buy this thing unless we added this feature," or, "If we only added this flavor they'd buy more from us." Then market research came along and said, "We know all because we did focus groups and surveys." Lately, the web analytics people came in and said, "Oh, but we've got search data and behavioral data so we really know what's on their minds."

Tomorrow, those who harness the gift of listening will be in the position of power. They will channel the Voice of the Customer and make it possible for the marketplace to be a conversation once again.

To what end? That depends—and is the subject of the next chapter.

CHAPTER 7

Getting Results—Driving Business Outcomes

Remember Chapter 1: Getting Focused—Identifying Goals? The Big Three Goals are very important, but it's time to get just a little more granular. The bottom line is great for the quarterly report, but it's not so good for navigation, which requires constant sightings and adjustments. The old saw about keeping an eye out the windshield instead of only on the rearview mirror is applicable.

Business outcomes are the results that help improve the bottom line. They are the indicators that provide feedback on whether you are likely to meet your goals or not.

♦ You can't have profits without income.

♦ You can't have income without customers.

♦ You can't have customers without prospective customers.

♦ You can't have prospects without suspects.

♦ You can't have suspects without awareness.

Desired business outcomes are measurable and include things like:

- Awareness—How many people know about your company or offering?

- Survey completions—How many were willing to answer your questions?

- Subscriptions—How many signed up for your newsletter, blog, or tweets?

- Registrations—How many wanted to be a member of your club?

- Blog comments—How many were engaged in conversation?

- Blog posts—How many mentioned you to others?

- Leads—How many are potential customers?

- Purchases—How many actually bought something from you?

Which outcomes are important to you depends on what you sell.

If you're a publisher, your goal is pretty clear. You want as many eyeballs looking at as many pages as possible. So you want to measure the number of people who show up at your web site and stick around. You want them to increase the amount of inventory you have to sell. If all goes well, you might also get them to subscribe to your paper periodical.

If you sell online, you want to delve into the prodigious panoply of web metrics including navigation, persuasion, and conversion.

A membership organization like a trade association might want to calculate how well their social media efforts are bringing in new members and volunteers.

A political campaign is looking to change minds and influence elections.

Regardless of which business outcomes you are hoping, planning, and working for, bear in mind that social media results take time. In his WebMetricsGuru blog, social media researcher Marshall Sponder warns that it can take months—many months—for social media campaigns to show results.

Marshall surveyed a number of social marketing experts and practitioners for his post at www.webmetricsguru .com/archives/2009/09/social-media-campaigns-take-time-3-months-1-year-for-results/ in which he recommends that you plan on spending six to twelve months of effort and data collection before you can tell whether you have hit a jackpot by fluke or have actually built a long-term, brand building program.

That still leaves us with the question: What are the most important things to measure?

Key Performance Indicators for Web Sites

If you want a deep dive into granular web site metrics, there's no better resource than Eric T. Peterson's *Big Book of Key Performance Indicators* (Figure 7.1) (www .webanalyticsdemystified.com/about_kpi_book.asp).

Eric describes KPIs this way:

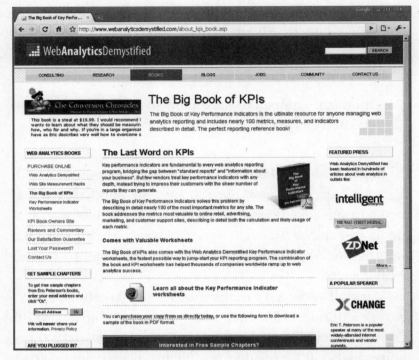

Figure 7.1   *The Big Book of KPIs* was the first and still seminal list of Things to Measure.

> *Key performance indicators are a response to a general organizational fear of big, ugly spreadsheets and complex applications. The big idea behind KPIs is that you're taking technical data and presenting it using business-relevant language. Key performance indicators:*

> ♦ *Use rates, ratios, percentages, and averages instead of raw numbers*

> ♦ *Leverage tachometers and thermometers and stoplights instead of pie charts and bar graphs*

♦ *Provide temporal context and highlight change instead of presenting tables of data*

♦ *Drive business-critical action*

The last point is the most important, that all good key performance indicators drive action. I'll say it again since it's worth repeating: All good key performance indicators drive action. This is the polite way of saying, "Any KPI that, when it changes suddenly and unexpectedly does not inspire someone to send an e-mail, pick up the phone, or take a quick walk to find help, is not a KPI worth reporting."

The Big Book of Key Performance Indicators starts with averages:

Average Page Views per Visit

Average Visits per Visitor

Average Time to Respond to E-mail Inquiries

Average Cost per Visitor

Average Cost per Visit

Average Cost per Conversion

Average Revenue per Visitor

It moves on to percentages:

Percent New and Returning Visitors

Percent New and Returning Customers

Percent Visitors in a Specific Segment

Percentage of High, Medium, and Low Time Spent Visits (Interest Categories)

Percentage of High, Medium, and Low Click Depth Visits (Interest Categories)

Then it dives into rates and ratios:

Order Conversion Rate

Buyer Conversion Rate

New and Returning Visitor Conversion Rate

New and Returning Buyer Conversion Rate

Ratio of New to Returning Visitors

Order Conversion Rate per Campaign

Cart Start Rate

Cart Completion Rate

Then it gets really interesting, when he breaks them out by business type:

Key Performance Indicators for Online Retailers

Key Performance Indicators for Content Sites

Key Performance Indicators for Marketing Sites

Key Performance Indicators for Customer Support Sites

As you can guess, I strongly recommend this book for the level of detail and the level-headedness used to describe them and their practical use.

Are there KIP's for social media? Some are starting to emerge. Take for example, the Econsultancy blog post by Chris Lake at http://econsultancy.com/blog/4887-35-social-media-kpis-to-help-measure-engagement called "35 social media KPIs to help measure engagement." Chris offers some clear insights about social media measurement and then provides the following:

A List of Social Interaction Metrics/KPIs

1. *Alerts (register and response rates/by channel/CTR/post click activity)*

2. *Bookmarks (onsite, offsite)*

3. *Comments*

4. *Downloads*

5. *Email subscriptions*

6. *Fans (become a fan of something/ someone)*

7. *Favourites (add an item to favourites)*

8. *Feedback (via the site)*

9. *Followers (follow something/someone)*

10. *Forward to a friend*

11. *Groups (create/join/total number of groups/group activity)*

12. *Install widget (on a blog page, Facebook, etc.)*

13. *Invite/Refer (a friend)*

14. *Key page activity (post-activity)*

15. *Love/Like this (a simpler form of rating something)*

16. *Messaging (onsite)*

17. *Personalisation (pages, display, theme)*

18. *Posts*

19. *Profile (e.g., update avatar, bio, links, email, customisation, etc.)*

20. *Print page*

21. *Ratings*

22. *Registered users (new/total/active/ dormant/churn)*

23. *Report spam/abuse*

24. *Reviews*

25. *Settings*

26. *Social media sharing/participation (activity on key social media sites, e.g. Facebook, Twitter, Digg, etc.)*

27. *Tagging (user-generated metadata)*

28. *Testimonials*

29. *Time spent on key pages*

30. *Time spent onsite (by source/by entry page)*

31. *Total contributors (and % active contributors)*

32. *Uploads (add an item, e.g. articles, links, images, videos)*

33. *Views (videos, ads, rich images)*

34. *Widgets (number of new widgets users/ embedded widgets)*

35. *Wishlists (save an item to wishlist)*

While monitoring web site behavior has become a well-respected art/science, social media KPIs are, by necessity, a little fuzzier. Yes, we want to know if we're improving our brand's standing. (Are they aware of us and do they like us?) Yes, we want to track every interaction through onsite behavior. (Are they lost? Are they completing their tasks?) Yes, we want to keep our finger on the pulse of what they are saying to us directly. (Is customer satisfaction improving?) But everybody—whether they realize it or not—is in the business of creating and fostering a community out there in Social Media Land.

Key Listening Indicators

Community is where most formal, organized, deliberate corporate social media efforts run off the rails. Good intentions, best practices, and project timelines are great tools, but building a community is a human endeavor. Social media is social first and media second. As advertising it's dead last. Face it, not everybody throws a great party.

Patrick O'Keefe has been professionally developing web sites since 1998 and could write a book about managing online forums. Fortunately, he *did* write a book on the subject called *Managing Online Forums: Everything You Need to Know to Create and Run Successful*

Community Discussion Boards (AMACOM, April 10, 2008) (www.managingonlineforums.com).

Yes, he covers the technical niceties, the legal issues, and designing and launching your community. But he also spends some time on developing and enforcing guidelines, choosing and managing moderators, involving your users, and keeping the site interesting and inviting.

His point in these areas is that a good moderator or community manager is more important than all the rest. Great technology and a fascinating subject can't overcome the ennui that sets in when the facilitator isn't up to the task.

All of the trials and tribulations for herding human cats in an online forum are hugely magnified when trying to corral all of them out there on all of those social platforms, blogs, discussion groups, Twitter accounts, and whatever got invented last week in a college dormitory.

Generally speaking, we are back in the realm of brand metrics. What does Nielsen Buzzmetrics (Figure 7.2) (http://en-us.nielsen.com/tab/product_families/nielsen_buzzmetrics) have to say about the health of your brand?

More specifically, we are heading into the realm of "listening platforms." At least, that's what Forrester Research calls them. "The Forrester Wave: Listening Platforms, Q1 2009," by principal analyst Suresh Vittal stated that listening platforms were still in their infancy. "While vendors aspire to deliver strategic insights to support the marketing organizations, they are often stuck in the world of tracking, monitoring, and delivering dashboards centered on operational metrics like mentions, reach, and discussion volume."

They reviewed eight leading listening platform vendors and discovered three areas that needed improvement:

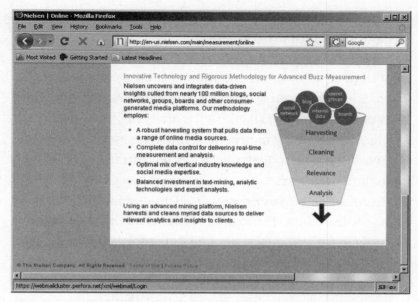

Figure 7.2   Nielsen Buzzmetrics offers themselves up as the social media brand benchmark.

sentiment analysis, integration with other metrics and systems, and experienced analytics professionals who could help get these tools and processes implemented.

In a nutshell, the tools declared too many comments "neutral" to be useful or trustworthy. It's a safe assumption that only the most delighted and most annoyed customers are engaged in a conversation and therefore very unlikely that their comments would be neutral. Without trust, the tools, indeed the listening platform concept, cannot succeed.

Like web analytics before it, these sets of tools are starting off in their own little worlds. Listening tools are going to have to participate and integrate with web analytics behavioral data, customer satisfaction survey data, and audience measurement services like Nielsen Netratings, comScore, and Hitwise. By itself, listening information is interesting;

combined with other customer-related information, it becomes a competitive weapon.

All of this is going to take some help by some smart and experienced people. At the moment, all we have is smart. Topic identification, sentiment and influence coding, and market segmentation all take a fair amount of trial and error, and as long as every company is in experimentation mode, we won't be able to learn as fast as we can from those who have done it before.

In another Forrester report, "Understanding the Total Cost of Listening Platforms," Suresh advises companies to budget for expenses beyond the tools. "Listening is a laborious task requiring employee support from within the marketing team and successful listening initiatives necessitate a clear designation of roles." This is a job for professionals. Just as marketing people have discovered that market research is not just a simple matter of floating a Survey Monkey questionnaire, listening is not something that your typical marketer—or market researcher—can do in their spare time.

As with all data-rich systems, the data can be automatically captured and even cleansed to turn it into information. Business rules can be applied to determine which chunks of information are more important, but knowledge comes only with experience and insight comes only after applying that knowledge through analysis. The endgame is coming up with insights, and that is a rare talent.

Listening is a challenge, but the tools and the professional analytical services are maturing. However, we need to measure more than just the tone of the marketplace. The marketplace is a conversation and that means we need to measure our impact on it. The challenge is to measure whether your team is doing a good job nurturing a loosely affiliated group of humans in an electronic communication environment.

Key Community Indicators

Web strategist Jeremiah Owyang (www.web-strategist.com) explains how measurement has become or *should be* a priority for online communities in a comment posted on February 25, 2009 (www.web-strategist.com/blog/2009/01/28/community-managers-must-deliver-roi-tips-for-surviving-a-recession).

"Community managers must educate stakeholders and management," Jeremiah says. Community managers have to be in the thick of it and stay connected, but they also have to be able to quickly communicate changes back to internal company stakeholders. That means metrics.

Forum One Communications floated their Online Community Metrics survey (www.onlinecommunityreport.com/uploads/metrics.pdf) in February of 2007. Fifty came back out of 150, an applause-worthy response rate in anybody's book. They asked a number of questions of online community professionals, including "Which community metrics do you track?"

Among the top metrics, the most important were:

Unique Visitors

New Member Registrations

Page Views

Retention/Attrition

Member Loyalty

Member Satisfaction

Most Active Members

Among the other key metrics not listed in the multiple choice answer above were:

Quality of content and exchange: For instance, resolution time, days thread was active, ratio of validated responses. Support communities are leading the way on best practices and reporting.

Tracking the brand through the "Community Ecosystem": Tracking brands and community members as they travel through the larger community ecosystem that spans sites, technologies, and devices.

Impact of the community on revenue: Particular attention is being paid to the value of members, both to the host communities' revenue and the organization's sales or fundraising.

Mobile interactions with the community: including views and posts from mobiles.

RSS subscriptions: RSS had surprisingly few mentions, which could speak to the relative difficulty of tracking RSS metrics, or the relative value of RSS metrics to community hosts.

Clearly, we have plenty to measure. According to Jeremiah Owyang, critical community metrics include:

♦ Improvement in marketing efficiency (word-of-mouth velocity)

♦ Reduction in support costs (deflected contact center or in-store incidents)

♦ Actual improvement to sales (yes, sales count!)

As for that last one, says Jeremiah, "If you can demon-strate this (like Dell's million dollar sales in Twitter), tout this loudly to management."

That post was prompted in part by a white paper pub-lished by Lithium Technologies (www.lithium.com) in the same month. Lithium offered up a Community Health Index as a new standard. What does a healthy community look like in their eyes?

After finishing up a "detailed, time-series analysis of up to a decade's worth of proprietary data that repre-sents billions of actions, millions of users, and scores of communities," Lithium suggests we should be measuring growth, usefulness, popularity, responsiveness, interactiv-ity, and liveliness. Some of those sound a great deal alike, so I'll let the paper (http://pages.lithium.com/community-health-index.html) speak for itself:

The characteristics of healthy communities and their corresponding health factors are:

Growing = Members

After an initial surge of registrations characteristic of a newly launched community, membership in a healthy community continues to grow. Although mature communities typically experience a slower rate of growth, they still add new members as the company's customer base grows. The traditional method for measuring membership is the registra-tion count.

Useful = Content

A critical mass of content posted on an online com-munity is clearly one of its strongest attractions to both members and casual visitors. In support communities, the content enables participants to arrive at a general understanding or get answers to specific questions. In engagement (enthusiast or marketing) communities, it serves as a magnet to attract and engage members. In listening communities, the content posted by community members gives the company valuable input from the customers who use their products or services.

A steady infusion of useful content, then, is essential to the health of a community. The traditional metric for measuring content is number of posts. This metric alone, however, gives no indication of the usefulness of the content, especially in communities that do not use content rating or tagging. In order to model content usefulness instead of sheer bulk, we consider page views as a surrogate for marketplace demand, but then dampen their effect to reduce the likelihood of spurious inflation.

Popular = Traffic

Like membership, traffic in a community— page views or eyes on content—is one of the most frequently cited metrics for community health. In deriving the Traffic health factor, we started with the standard page view metric, but then mitigated the effect of robot crawlers in order to diminish their impact.

Responsiveness

The speed with which community members respond to each other's posts is another key metric for determining community health. Participants in support communities, for example, are only willing to wait for answers for a limited amount of time. The same is true for engagement and other types of communities. If there is too much of a lag between posts and responses, conversations peter off and members start looking elsewhere.

The traditional response time metric counts the number of minutes between the first post and the first reply. That first post might be anything—a question, a blog article, an idea, a status update. Because our analysis of community-member behavior has revealed the importance of subsequent responses, we have enhanced the traditional response time metric to account for all of the responses in a topic.

Interactive = Topic Interaction

Interaction between participants is one of the key reasons that online communities exist. The traditional metric for measuring interaction is thread depth, where threads are topics of discussion and their depth is the average number of posts they contain. This way of looking at interaction, however, does not consider the number of individuals who are participating. As a result, a topic with six posts by the same participant would have the same depth as one with six different contributors. Because our experience with online communities has led us to understand that the number of participants in an interaction is even more important than the number of posts, we have added the dimension of unique contributors to our calculation of Topic Interaction.

Liveliness

Although most people would be hard-pressed to define it, they recognize and respond to liveliness or buzz when they encounter it. Research has shown that participants are not only attracted to but are also motivated to return and contribute in communities that feel animated and vibrant.

We find that liveliness can be best measured by tracking a critical threshold of posting activity that experience and analysis have shown us characterizes healthy communities. In calculating the Liveliness factor, we look not only at the number of posts but also at their distribution within the community.

The culmination of the previous list is a dashboard (Figure 7.3) that tells you at a glance if your community is balanced.

There are a couple of frameworks out there to point the way. The simplest is basic Return on Investment. In their book *Groundswell: Winning in a World Transformed by Social Technologies*, Charlene Li and Josh Bernoff outline a specific case from toy company Lego engaging Lego Ambassadors.

Cost items (estimated: $200K)

> Internet coordination
>
> Staff time
>
> Travel
>
> Payment in Lego bricks

Benefits (estimated: $500K increase in sales)

> 25 Ambassadors reach 100 Adult Fans of Lego (AFOL) each: 2,500 people

Figure 7.3 Lithium's Community Health Index shows the six health factors they feel deserve your attention.

Each AFOL buys an average of $1K of Lego products/year

Expected increase due to Ambassadors' efforts: 20 percent

Adult Fans of Lego represent 5 percent to 10 percent of Lego's billion-dollar-plus business. Lego Ambassadors program was created to:

Build relationships with the most enthusiastic AFOLs

Help Lego learn what's happening in the highly connected AFOL world

In hard numbers, the case in compelling.

Compared with the Competition

How good are you at this whole social media thing anyway?

1. We're good.

2. We're great!

3. We're learning.

4. We stink.

If you choose anything except #3, you're wrong. To be more accurate, you don't know. The proper response to that question is "Compared to what?"

Wetpaint (www.wetpaint.com) is something like a web site development platform. Actually, it's a web presence platform. "Wetpaint lets you build a rich, online community around the whatever-it-is that you're really into. Utilizing the best features of wikis, blogs, forums, and social networks, Wetpaint mixes everything you need so you can create, collect, and organize content on your own social web site." They decided to think deeply about social media and determine who's good at it—and publish the results on something they call the Engagement Database (www.engagementdb.com).

The Engagement Database is a wonderfully visual look at who's any good at this community thing (Figure 7.4).

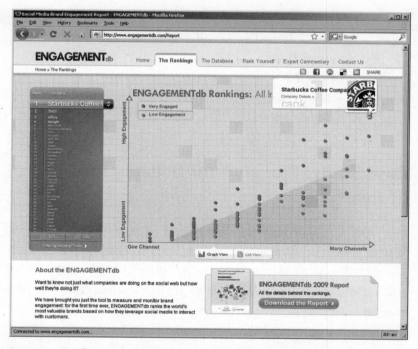

Figure 7.4 According to Engagementdb, Starbucks is more involved in social media than the rest.

You can do a quick self-assessment against the Engagementdb based on what social media tools you use (blogs, calendars, bookmarking services, social networking sites, etc.), how active your customers are on the social media tools you use, how responsive your company is to customer activity, whether you have lots of people involved with lots of investment and broad interest across the company or it's just you, and finally, what type of business you're in. That's just for fun. The database itself is a bit more complex.

The good people at Wetpaint evaluated and scored each brand's engagement in various channels using criteria customized for that particular type of social media. They looked at how deeply involved different departments and executives were and added all the channel sub-scores together to get a brand's overall engagement score.

Is it accurate?

Is it complete?

Is it a global standard?

Compared to what?

Case Study: Blogging for Dollars—The Cost of Reach

Sea World San Antonio launched a new thrill ride called Journey to Atlantis and set out to promote it via roller coaster bloggers. They wanted to build relationships with the coaster community in order to build awareness of the ride in order to get more people to the park.

They targeted 22 coaster enthusiast bloggers, treated them as a VIP audience, and created 11 videos and a 45-photo portfolio of the ride's construction for the bloggers to use at will. They invited the bloggers and the American Coaster Enthusiast forum to the media launch day and let them have the first ride.

How well did it work?

- Half the targeted bloggers wrote about the ride and linked to it.

- They got another 50 links from unique web sites.

- The American Coaster Enthusiasts group brought 30 of its members to the ride.

OK—that's nice. But what about business outcomes? A survey at the park determined that, at a cost of $44,000, the overall cost per impression was $0.22 versus $1.00 for television. Further, those who came because of what they saw online made up over $2.6 million in revenue.

If you're looking for ammunition to convince people in your company that social media and social media metrics are a good thing, stop right there. If you want to dig deep into this case study from an analyst's perspective, it'll be worth your while to read the Econsultancy commentary called "A Social Media Marketing Campaign Deconstructed" at http://econsultancy.com/blog/2363-a-social-media-marketing-campaign-deconstructed.

Case Study: Social Media Metrics at Intuit

I met with a fascinating and analytically creative cross-functional team at Intuit that included Dylan Lewis, group manager of web analytics, Sue West, group manager of research, Christine Morrison., social media marketing, and Seth Greenberg, director of digital marketing. Who said measuring social media was a lonely job? Here, it takes a village.

Sentimental Journey

Intuit uses Radian6 to do weekly reporting on reach, influence, and sentiment, particularly during tax season. One of their clever twists is tracking five categories of sentiment ranging from:

1. Recommendation ("You should get it!")

2. Positive but not recommending ("Oh, I love Turbo-Tax.")

3. Neutral, in passing ("I use TurboTax." or just "I installed TurboTax.")

4. Negative ("I hate TurboTax.")

5. Really Negative (The F-bomb or "I'm taking Intuit to court.")

And the tool they used to assign sentiment and tag the comments? The same one as the *Washington Post*—they hired a human. A contractor was brought in and he literally read through every single post—almost 40,000 posts about Intuit and their competitors from January 1 to April 15.

A week over week trend analysis bubbled up what's hot over the weekend so product managers and public relations managers could take note. As a first-time effort, it proved very valuable although the team admitted the process might not be sustainable. On the other hand, none of them felt artificial intelligence was going to come to their aid any day soon.

They did give it a shot, however. They ran all 40,000 comments through the text analytics program they use for reviewing customer care. It was helpful, but it couldn't give them what they were hoping for and turns out to be a fairly labor intensive process itself.

They start by teaching the text analytics system keywords and phrases. They developed their own categories and models. That takes time, but once done, they have something that's stable and sustainable. But the true value comes from categorization. A comment may be positive in terms of ease of use, value for money, great support, etc.

This way the analyst can look at all positive comments then see the distribution of positive comments based on the category to get a feel for what percentage of customers feel the product is easy to use. The real value comes from drilling down and reading the actual verbatim comments. For diagnosing a particular issue or uncovering a sore spot, it's a great tool.

PROMOTIONAL CONSIDERATION

In 2008, Intuit ran a contest called SuperStatus. They put out a series of 30 mini challenges and people had to answer the challenge by updating their status either in their Facebook account, their MySpace account, or their Twitter account. They had to include some particular, trackable keyword in their status for verification.

Sounds like a great idea but measuring the effectiveness was a challenge. They knew how many people had entered the contest but ran into a conundrum when trying to figure out whether they were changing people's opinions.

This is when Christine (social media marketing) went to Sue (group manager of research) and asked for help. This turned out to be a masterstroke. Sue has been doing classical market research for years and is widely respected across the organization. When Sue talks, people listen.

Sue applied traditional research methodology in a social setting. She surveyed people about their familiarity with the Intuit brand, brand image, and purchase intent—the typical market research types of things. But then they asked people to send a link to the questionnaire to their friends.

Not only was Intuit able to understand who their contest participants were, what their tax prep methods were, how participating in this challenge might have changed their perceptions of TurboTax, they also reached out to their friends and friends of friends to monitor the power each one had to influence their friends.

Now they had a brand-building contest that also helped them understand the number of friends who were exposed to the campaign and how that might have changed the way they looked at TurboTax *plus* their actual behavior during tax season—behavior in terms of what tax preparation software or service they used.

The project went very well. Compared to what? In that traditional marketing research way that she does so well, Sue compared their contest entrants with a control group. They created a segment of people who were frequent participants of social network contests. Of people who like to participate in online contests, they calculated a brand image lift of eight points. These people were not just playing to win, they were getting the message and having their minds changed about the brand.

They measured against brand statements like:

This is a brand I trust.

Value for money.

Worth paying more for an easy way to get a big refund.

It does the work for me.

It gives me confidence to do my own taxes.

It's the easiest way to prepare my taxes.

The results showed a lift range between 9 points and 14 points on each individual brand metric compared with the control.

The icing on the cake was a 10-point lift in purchase intent. Impressive numbers by any measure.

The sprinkles on top of the icing was that for the first time ever, they could report back to the organization and there wasn't a single raised eyebrow. There wasn't a single question about the tactics, the medium of the outcome. They respected Sue and understood the methodology. There was just no pushback.

SHOW ME THE MONEY

Brand is grand. Awareness is compareless. Intent is heaven sent. But what about sales? Intuit is now ready to build out the sales funnel for the next go-round.

The funnel starts off with total awareness, unaided and aided, familiarity with the brand, and the brand image attributes above. Purchase intent is next followed by actual purchase. They asked the basic research question "How did you hear about us?"

Next time, given experience and foresight, they are prepared to do a pre- and a post-analysis to get an even more rigorous control group.

THE HOLY GRAIL

As the director of digital marketing, Seth has his eyes on the data integration prize. "I manage five channels: paid search, organic search, display advertising, affiliate programs, and social media. I want to know how social interacts with display, how display interacts with search, and how is social really helping across all these channels as well and vice versa?"

The Holy Grail of attribution is never far from any manager who is doing well in some areas and okay in others. Once the ball is rolling, it's natural to want to know about the interaction among all of them and how they interact with traditional, offline media.

THE TRICKY BIT

Intuit is a clued-in organization. The number and caliber of people they have addressing these issues is impressive. They are not shy about using the best tools on the market. They like exploring new possibilities. But Seth is concerned about one area.

"I think we're pretty good in terms of measuring stuff," he says. "But sometimes that hinders us. Sometimes it stifles some of the creativity in how far we want to strive for. For example, Citizen Kane, which was directed by Orson Welles, is a masterpiece because he didn't know what the heck he was doing. He kept pushing for things from the cinematographer you were not supposed to ask for. When we start understanding how to measure stuff, we start putting limitations on the creative side. Instead of trying to reach for the stars and then figure out how to measure it."

That's why we'll always need 20-year-olds. They don't know what can't be done.

Haven't We Already Solved This Problem?

Katie Delahaye Paine (KDPaine & Partners) has been personally associated with every serious effort to develop public relations measurement standards for longer than would be gentlemanly of me to say. In 1996, after a heated discussion at a Public Relations Society of America conference, she was on the team that wrote the first Institute for Public Relations white paper, "Guidelines and Standards for Measuring the Effectiveness of PR Programs and Activities." (www .instituteforpr.org/research_single/measuring_activities)

These days, Katie is focused on outcomes as the critical metric, and she divides the business outcomes of

PR into four basic categories, which are summarized in Table 7.1 on the next page:

1. Financial

2. Reputation

3. Employee

4. Public policy

No company can afford to act like an aircraft carrier. No matter how large your firm is, you must be agile and respond quickly to shifting winds and rising waters.

The magic of online marketing is the ease with which you can alter your message, your offer, and your target audience. The curse of online marketing is the speed with which you must alter your message, your offer, and your target audience. Properly, relentlessly, and promptly tracking the impact of your social media marketing is the only way to get the visibility you need to appropriately adjust your course.

Before we close out on measuring results, there's one more item that's off the beaten track—something that is worth going after and a lot trickier than the rest to measure: brilliant ideas.

Table 7.1 KDPAine & Partners list of PR business outcomes and their metrics covers the subject

	Business Outcome	**Measurement Method**
Financial outcomes	Marketing public relations drives sales. Investor public relations drives investment.	Consumer response: Field survey of consumers, determine purchase levels and exposure to PR results, isolate causal effects through statistical analysis.
	Public relations drives donations and membership for relevant organizations.	Market Mix Modeling/Econometric Modeling: Gather PR output/outcome data in conjunction with other marketing activity by market, by marketing function, by region, by time period and factor by revenue-generation by market, by region and over time. Apply regression analysis.
	Improves efficiency by better audience targeting. PR reaches more people with a credible message for less money.	Determine comparative cost of different communication approaches; calculate percent of target reached; determine change in purchase cycle resultant from PR activity.

Avoids catastrophic cost.

Mitigates impacts of crises.

Assess competitors and peers who may have faced similar crises, track emergence of their crises and impact on sales, stock price, and relevant business measures to evaluate the potential impact that was avoided.

Reputation

Increases likelihood to purchase/consider your brand(s).

Minimizes the effects of a crisis.

Reinforces communication of organizational values.

Rebuilds trust after a crisis.

Establishes credibility of new products/companies; ease of market entry.

Commanding higher prices, lower costs, premium on stock price.

Enhances recommendations/word-of-mouth leading to faster adoption.

Increases customer loyalty/renewals/satisfaction.

Benchmark reputation/relationship metrics via survey prior to a campaign, repeat every 3–6 months.

Correlate attitudinal studies with customer purchase attitude and behavior.

Map conversations (and tone) in traditional and social media to web analytic data (e.g., registrations, requests for information, sales leads, etc.).

Map conversations/reputation to financial analysts' opinions and stock price volatility.

Correlate share of thought leadership visibility to adoption of policy positions.

Table 7.1 (*continued*)

	Business Outcome	Measurement Method
	Improves the attracting/ retaining of talent. Lowers legal costs.	
Employee	Increases employee satisfaction and engagement, leading to greater efficiency, increased retention, lower turnover rates, lower recruitment costs, and higher productivity. Lowers legal costs. Changes employee behaviors such as greater levels of focus on key areas such as safety, quality, call response times. Provides greater transparency and commitment to and from employees. Creates a platform should it be necessary to communicate bad news at some stage in the future. *Note:* Items here can also refer to other internal publics such as trade association members.	Use control groups and compare to employee populations exposed to PR activities. Focus on performance outcomes not attitude or awareness. Match/correlate messaging data to: • Employee satisfaction and engagement findings • Employee turnover statistics and other recruitment data • Call response times • Customer experience surveys Consider other research tools and data—focus groups, exit interview data, days of sickness, etc. *Note:* Items here can also refer to other internal publics such as trade association members.

Public policy	Creates public awareness, understanding, and support for legislation, regulation, and political candidates. Affects voter behavior. Helps pass legislation, regulation, and initiatives. Affects specific companies and industries through appropriations, tax impacts, and regulatory changes that can affect any and all aspects of a business. Instigates and perpetuates grassroots or grasstops campaigns.	Use available public tracking services at national (e.g., major network polls) or local (e.g., university polling centers) to track changes in awareness, understanding, support, and voter intent. Also where possible link to level of PR activity. Conduct tracking survey of key politicians or regulators. Can often use Influentials' awareness as a proxy for elected officials, as well as to measure the "edge" of a trend. Post-election surveys can isolate specific effects of PR by determining actual voting behavior, as well as levels of exposure to different communication media. Actual public or legislator voting behavior.

Crowdsourcing

The customer is always right.

The customer is king.

The customer comes first.

Find a need and fill it.

Find out what they want and sell it to them.

All of the above is true and good—as far as it goes. It only goes as far as The iPod Conundrum. The iPod conundrum is simply this: Your customers are never going to help you invent the Next Big Thing. As Henry Ford liked to say, if he had asked people what they wanted, they would have said, "Faster horses."

But that time-honored piece of wisdom has another twist to it in these days of crowdsourcing. Just as it sounds, this is the art of asking enough people for their input that somebody, somewhere does *invent* an iPod. Or at least leads your team in that direction.

For Vida Killian at Dell's IdeaStorm, measuring the number of people, comments, and votes is a way to tell if the system is working. But measuring great ideas, actionable ideas, breakthrough ideas—that's where the payoff is.

No one needs to convince you of the value that mass incentives can have in spurring innovation in science and technology (www.theglobeandmail.com/news/technology/article754494.ece).

Almost 10 years ago, a Canadian mining company unlocked their data vault and let anybody and everybody plunder 45 years of proprietary information about one of their less-than-stellar mines and geological data about the nearby area. This mine had a lowly annual gold production of 50,000 ounces at a relatively high cost of $360 per ounce. So they asked the world's geologists to take a crack at it. The idea was open source mining analysis and a half a million dollars was put on the table for the winner.

The challenge was to find the best way to find 6 million ounces of gold in an area a little under 80 square miles. More than a thousand geologists submitted plans and the top three took the prizes. But the winner was US Gold Corp. and Lexam Explorations Inc. They are now unearthing 500,000 ounces of gold a year at a cost of $60 per ounce. Crowdsourcing worked well for them.

You can use crowdsourcing for product ideas, customer service, television ads, usability studies, it doesn't matter. Just be sure you have a standard method to measure the response and the outcome. If it goes viral, that's great—but if it produces no results then it was just a PR stunt and even then it may not have improved your company's image.

Measuring the value of ideas is a very long-term prospect, even longer than customer lifetime value.

So where do we stand?

♦ You've got goals.

♦ You've got a way to measure your audience reach.

♦ You've got a way to identify and measure influence.

♦ You've got a way to recognize and measure sentiment.

♦ You've got a way to listen and measure what you hear.

♦ You've got a way to measure response and business outcomes.

All you need to do now is convince the people with their hands on the budget that this is a good idea.

CHAPTER 8
Getting Buy-In—Convincing Your Colleagues

I've spent the last 30 years explaining why computers are so incredible.

I've spent the last 15 years explaining why marketing online is so incredible. I've spent the last 10 years explaining why measuring all of this stuff is so valuable.

I've learned a few things about explaining and a few things about measuring marketing.

First and foremost, humans do not like being measured. If you walk into my office with a graph, a chart, and a spreadsheet in your hand, I know instinctively that you're there to judge me. "Accountability" is another word for "we don't trust you so we're going to measure everything you do."

That's the unspoken problem. The spoken one was hammered home to me by Kim Johnston, vice president of global sales and marketing operations at Symantec Corporation after a killer presentation at the eMetrics Marketing Optimization Summit in Washington, D.C.

This computer science major turned math economics graduate was running her marketing department by the numbers. But she still got excited about branding and loves

199

the creative side's ability to connect the product value to the hearts and minds of her customers.

The ah-ha moment for me and many in the audience (the response was audible) was a diagram she showed of all the marketing campaigns running for just one of their products. It included online ads, e-mail marketing, Incredible Hulk co-branded arcade games, in-store advertising, TIVO-tizing, an 18-wheeler demo truck, private movie screenings, and a whole lot more. It was one of those unreadable slides that left you with the impression that it was all a little too complex to be managed by mere mortals.

Kim said she looked at all the promotions that were not delivering measurable results and cut them. She then cut all the projects that were not being measured. The new diagram showed almost half of the programs had vanished. The result? More than a 20 percent lift in response for the same dollar. The reasoning is unassailable. The numbers speak for themselves. The political ability to pull it off? Priceless.

But what really got me was a bit of insight she shared after her presentation when I got her alone for a spirited conversation. I asked her my favorite question: What's the hard part?

Turns out it's the same at Symantec as it is at almost every other company I work with—getting people to undertake the whole measurement process. But here, it was for a different reason. We talked about the human aversion to being measured. That queasy feeling of people scoring how much they like you on a scale of 1 to 10. But Kim's problem is even bigger, more ingrained, and probably more prevalent than I had imagined. "My people are okay with the idea and are actually hungry for the numbers but it's just one more damned thing," she told me. "They're slammed trying to get their best work out the door as it is."

Besides doing more with less, we're asking people to add a page tag here and a reporting mechanism there, and it's just one more straw on the camel's back. Everything we can do to make the counting and reporting a little easier will boost productivity, increase results, and allow the marketing department a little more time to do that which drew them into the business in the first place: Be creative. It doesn't take a degree in math economics to figure that out—but it helps.

Is massive change the sort of thing you can only do when you're at the very top of an organization? No. But you do have to convince the dinosaurs, er, executives at the top that this is important.

Senior managers are not dumb, but they are slow to understand and embrace new communications methods.

Chances are excellent that your boss and his boss and her boss did not grow up with Internet access. Maybe they didn't even have it at college. Here are a few steps you need to take to convince them that social media is not only inevitable and not only a vital part of your marketing mix, but it is a pathway to profits.

Step One: Accept Your Role as Change Agent

Steve Covey, author of *The 7 Habits of Highly Effective People* (Simon & Schuster) likes trim tabs.

A trim tab is a rudder's rudder. It's very hard to turn a very large rudder when you want to turn a very large ship. So they put a little movable rudderette at the bottom of the rudder: a trim tab. The trim tab can be moved with much less effort but it provides the leverage that moves the big rudder that moves the ship. Your job, should you decide to accept it, is to be the trim tab that moves the executives that move the company.

It takes a bit of doing. You're approaching a massive, old, bureaucratic institution with deeply felt and widely held beliefs that everything they've done is right and should continue to be done that way. Your job is to tell them that things have changed. This may take some time. You may feel it's an impossible task and that your company simply moves too slow for anything productive to come from trim-tabbing within your lifetime.

If you were looking to be an independent consultant anyway, then simply e-mail the following memo (adapted from *Customer Service on the Internet, Second Edition by some guy named Jim Sterne*) to your chief executive:

Good morning, Mr. Van Winkle,

While you were dozing, the world took a few turns around the sun—in the other direction. While you were calculating your portfolio's net present value on your abacus while listening to various toadies telling you only what you wanted to hear and insisting that your PR department could manage this social media stuff, the business landscape became a business conversationscape. It's a Connected World After All.

While you thought you were safe behind your walls with a phalanx of defensive administrati keeping the rabble at bay, the walls became opaque and have turned transparent. The rabble can see you now. They can see you prevaricate. They watch you vacillate. They see your attention fluctuate. They know if you've been bad or good so communicate for goodness sake.

Those little people, waaay down there, that you dismiss as mere customers are now eye-level with

*you and yours and are talking about you with-
out even waiting for you to turn your back.
They are taking their business to companies with
open-door, open-window, and open-season policies.
Other companies that are letting information flow
like water between trading partners.*

*Customers are voting with their wallets and the
results are starting to pour in: it's a rout. Our traditional competitors are figuring it out and are
doing their best to keep up with the new kids on the
block who are ignoring 50 years of business tradition and simply serving customers online. They are
blogging, they are tweeting, they are friending, and
they are reaping the relationships that will drive
business from this day forward.*

*Where's the problem, Mr. Van Winkle? The problem
is somewhere between you and me.*

*You didn't get where you are by sticking your head
in the sand for lo these many years. You read in-
flight magazines. You know which end of the pencil
has an eraser. But those guys in the middle, who
have spent decades building their fiefdoms brick-
by-brick on the backs of us worker-bees, are terrified
of change. They think if they let this social media
stuff grow to its full potential they might be out of
a job. The funny part is—they're right! And there's
nothing they can do to stop it.*

*So it's time to open the kimono, Rip. Time to wake
up and smell the customers. Time to admit that
this cranky old organization is not made up of the
best and the brightest. It's just made up of good old-
fashioned people. People who will do their best to*

*help their customers in every way they can, includ-
ing turning this stodgy old dust trap into the Visible
Corporation.*

*Please make it possible for customers to commu-
nicate with us via whatever channel they prefer.
Let them see that we are not perfect but that
we are dedicated to doing our best for them.
Stop hiding behind press releases and memoranda
and go meet people face-to-face and monitor-to-
monitor.*

*I have a few ideas about how we can do that down
here in the customer service department. If you'd
like to chat, you can *click here* to see my calendar,
which includes doctor appointments for company-
induced stress attacks and interviews with venture
capitalists about a little Internet start-up idea I've
been thinking about. My schedule is an open book.
See how well that works?*

*I hope to hear from you soon, because that really
is an iceberg dead ahead, and it really does have
our name on it.*

Your Obedient Servant,

Jim

BE READY TO LEAVE

Do you *really* want to be a change agent? Then pack your
bags.

A change agent is a person who believes so strongly that
they are right about how a company should operate that
they are willing to put everything on the line to make it
happen. Up to and including their job.

Be bold. Be boisterous. Be a pain in the neck. If it's not possible to Do the Right Thing, then maybe you don't want to work there anyway.

Not willing to have the Change Agent target painted on your back? That's okay. You can still follow the following advice. Just dial it down a little.

Step Two: Match the Message with the Receiver

Back in 1994, upper management really needed to understand what the Internet was all about before they could determine what it meant for business. So many people were shouting about the New Economy (think sticky eyeballs and no business model) that it was tough for business managers to sufficiently understand the fundamentals to make investment decisions with any logic.

If you want to get across the incredible value of social media and social media metrics, here's what you need to explain to your boss, depending on what type of boss you have.

TYPE A: THE CORPORATE UPPER CLASS, AND THOSE WHO PREFER STRATEGY TO TACTICS

What to tell them: Why, not how.

If you try to differentiate instant messaging from a direct tweet, their eyes will glaze over and they'll reach for their BlackBerries. Better to talk about the value of measuring and improving your customer communications rather than the specifics of how it all works. Do *not* explain how sentiment information can be extracted at the sentence, clause, or individual opinion expression level. Instead, explain how improved understanding will raise revenues, lower costs, and increase customer satisfaction.

TYPE B: DIVISION MANAGERS IN CONTROL OF YOUR PROJECT BUDGET

What to tell them: The process, not the products.

Making funding decisions requires thorough knowledge about what's going to be done, who's going to do it, how long it'll take, what it's likely to cost, and how much it's likely to earn or save. These people are not interested in the technical niceties of iPhone Twitter client tracking or the difference between Nielsen's Brand Affinity Maps and Telligent Analytics' external buzz monitoring. They just want to know that you can deliver a specific result, when it's going to happen, what it's going to cost, and how you're going to ensure it.

TYPE C: BUSINESS-ORIENTED DEPARTMENT MANAGERS TRYING TO USE THE RESULTING REPORTS

What to tell them: What it means and what to think about it.

A talented leader blessed with a talented staff can take input from that staff at face value. They trust their people to have analyzed the data and made well-considered recommendations. They want your honest opinion based on your best efforts. They're desperate to know what changes to make to their portion of the social media milieu to reach their goals, and they want you to save them from reading the graphs and charts your social media analytics tools spit out. Tell them what it means and what to think about it and they'll thank you.

Type D: Technically Oriented Department Managers Trying to Use the Resulting Reports

What to tell them: How it works, in gruesome detail, so they can make up their own minds.

The department manager who is more technically astute and less comfortable with how you came to your conclusions is a high-maintenance misfortune. They need the white paper, the book, the PowerPoint slides, and the workshop to firmly grasp the intricacies of social media and social media metrics so they can understand exactly how the reports were created and, therefore, what the data might mean. Let your vendors have some face time with these people and then crank out the desired reports. Do not hesitate to offer up insights, but be sure to show exactly which bits and bytes you relied on for your opinion.

Type E: Technical Managers

What to tell them: How it works, so they can determine the best technical solution.

Now it gets really sticky. You'll need to get your type Cs (business-oriented department managers) to clearly identify their goals so you can help your type Es (technical managers) figure out the best technical solution to capturing, analyzing, and reporting social data. If you have some type Ds (technically oriented department managers) who are willing to work hand-in-hand with your type Es, there's a decent chance you'll be able to find a number of social media metrics tools, services, and processes that meet your needs, instead of waiting until after implementation to find out they do not.

So create your multi-layered PowerPoint stack that will tell the whole story. But then figure out to whom you are pitching so you'll know which part of the story they need.

Step Three: Low-Hanging Fruit

"Prove it." Everybody you have to convince has the same objection. "Sounds great, Bob. But has anybody else done this before?"

The Web is full of great stories of wild success but people really want to see relevant examples that weren't flukes.

Remember what they asked you to help create a "Viral Marketing Program"? Remember having to talk them down? Remember how hard it was to get them to let go of that silver bullet? Well, they remember too and now they are slightly skeptical. So it's time to get them enthused again.

Case studies and success stories are great, but only when people can see themselves in the role of the hero. "And then he put on his red cape and flew into the fault line to stop the earthquake and save Lois from certain death" is a fun tale, but it doesn't resonate.

"Then we charted the number of mentions against the amount of blogging we did and mapped it out over time." Now that's something an individual could see themselves doing.

Other people's success stories are good, but if you really want to make an impression, find examples that are specific to your audience. The most important stories are the ones close to home about people and projects within your organization. "If Susan can do it, then so can I," they will think. Or perhaps, "If Henry does that again and I don't, he'll get the promotion and I won't." Now we're getting personal.

Step Four: Make It Personal

Understand the compensation packages of the people you are trying to convince. Show them the money.

No, you don't need to know how big their paycheck is. You just need to know how they'll reach their bonus. Once you understand their personal, nay private motivation, you understand what will make them sit up and take notice. Show them how social media metrics will help them toward their personal monetary goals.

Start with higher-level goals so they don't get spooked right out of the gate. Begin with organizational goals. Yes, we want to raise revenue, lower costs, increase satisfaction, and beat the pants off the competition in terms of the number of patents filed and cool T-shirts we hand out at trade shows. But which of these takes precedence?

A manager's paycheck is usually tied directly to specific changes in specific metrics over specific time periods within specific budgets. It's important that the individual you are trying to persuade has concrete numbers they can track with confidence.

Once you clarify the goals, the proper metrics will become apparent, as will the systems to capture the data necessary to track those metrics. Analyzing more and more detailed metrics can be a great help, until they reach that inevitable point of diminishing returns.

If their goal is to increase online sales, then measuring sales alone will not give them any visibility into the selling process. They'll want to track conversations and sentiment as well as clickthroughs, page views, and revenues.

If you throw too much data at them, if you produce too many reports, if they have too much information to consider, the cost of collecting, storing, analyzing, and reporting that information is, by definition, more expensive than the benefits they can derive from its use as a decision-making tool. So keep it simple.

But make it personal. And make sure your metrics are useful, rather than merely interesting.

Step Five: Bring a Plan

We're in new territory. That makes people nervous. There might be dragons. There might be Morlocks. There might be a place where the ship sails off the edge of the Earth. So bring a map. Even if your map is incomplete or sketchy, it provides something to hold on to.

Your map will depend on corporate culture.

CENTRAL OR DISTRIBUTED?

Some companies are distributed and some are hierarchical. All Internet projects started in a distributed manner because the individual who first created a web site, first posted a blog, or first tweeted did so without a net. They were mavericks acting on their own.

Later, they discovered others doing the same thing and they were thrilled to find allies in the cause. But individual efforts are not the most efficient. Suresh Vittal, principal analyst at Forrester Research, promotes the idea of shared learning. "With any big organization," Suresh says, "support groups are looking at this problem and saying, 'Well, if the toothpaste guy goes off and spends a million dollars and the shampoo guy goes off and spends a million dollars and the soap guy spends a million dollars, then we're going to create a central service team because the interaction affects their best practices. The service organization should not hinder the creative efforts but support their execution."

Should you open the doors to the social analytics tool-box, letting everybody do their own analysis and draw their own conclusions? Or should you retain tight control over the data and spoon-feed those who initially showed no or little interest in the process but are only looking for numbers to support their conclusion-du-jour?

The answer is yes; each in their own time.

The pendulum started off way over on the scattered side of the issue. It will help everybody if it's brought all the way to the centralization side. The analytics team must control the tool selection, implementation, and interpretation. There is so much to know and so many mistakes that can trip one up when social analytics is launched that the task should only be handed to trained drivers on a closed course wearing seatbelts and helmets.

Step by step, these experts can support the business units with golden nuggets of statistical truth and enthrall the uninitiated with their insights. Once the pupils are sufficiently hooked on the idea and the methods, senior management can be persuaded to invest more resources. At that point, centralization can begin in earnest.

The analysis team can recruit new members, upgrade the tools, and expand their purview. This is the time to establish processes and procedures, set standard definitions, and create a corporate understanding of how to draw the most valuable insights from the available data. The central team will reign supreme—for a while.

Eventually, the central team will not be needed as each business unit acquires a taste for the value of social media metrics and will develop the ability to go it alone. The processes will be streamlined, familiarity with the tools will improve, and critical thinking will become part and parcel of the marketing milieu. Each group will bake analytics into each project as a matter of course and all will be well—for a while.

Remember that pendulum?

Once that pendulum has swung all the way over to the decentralized side of the arc, there will be trouble afoot. Nothing is immutable and how people capture data, cleanse data, take measurements, and interpret the results will change over time. Why's that so bad? What's wrong with each business unit doing their own thing to optimize their own marketing in their own way? It drives the CMO crazy.

The CMO (or other sufficiently high-up individual) needs to be able to compare apples to apples. As soon as she sees that Group A's numbers do not line up with Group B's numbers, there will be hell to pay come budget allocation time.

Step Six: Read a Book

The topic of "change management" is much too big for this space. You can get a master's degree in change management and still have more to study. It's all about getting people to be willing to do something different.

Whether it's eat a different breakfast cereal or manage their organizations in a new way, change is unnerving. Humans like everything to be just so, so that they can relax. You want them to get outside their comfort zones. Sometimes that's a serious challenge.

Hard though it may be, doing new things and doing old things in new ways is essential when it comes to online marketing and measuring online marketing. The marketplace is a conversation, the customer is in control, and when it comes to change, you ain't seen nothin' yet . . . until you head on to the next chapter.

CHAPTER 9

Getting Ahead—Seeing the Future

Feeling a little overwhelmed? Hold on to your hat. Truth is stranger than fiction and a lot more interesting these days . . .

Everything Becomes Social

It's an old truism that anything important enough and valuable enough on a computer eventually gets pushed down onto the operating system. Windows Explorer acts like Internet Explorer if you type a URL into the address field at the top of the folder. Frequently used tools and protocols end up in the Accessories folder. Mac users laugh at all the different programs Windows users use when they simply have the features at their fingertips.

Social is one of those. There will be a Collaborate button on every application. There will be a Where Are They? button on every map. You will have the ability to see search results sorted by which ones your friends clicked on, and product reviews will be sorted by who you know rather than geography or recency. Knowing that your friend Jay really liked that movie but your friend Brian didn't contains

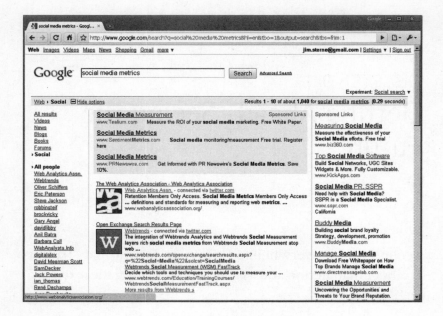

Figure 9.1   Google knows who my friends are.

much more information than if 85 percent of two million people liked or did not like it.

When I search for "Social Media Metrics" with Google's Social Search (in the Google Lab at the moment), I see "Results from people in your social circle" (Figure 9.1).

Every book you read will include comments from friends, comments from scholars, and comments from friendly scholars. Every movie you watch will include commentary by the director and the people in your quilting club. Everywhere you go you will have the option to bring along a few or a few thousand friends. Your telephone will be the device that identifies you and your location to those who want to inform. You will be able to meet-up, tweet-up, and synch-up anywhere at any time. Everybody will be connected to everybody (Figure 9.2).

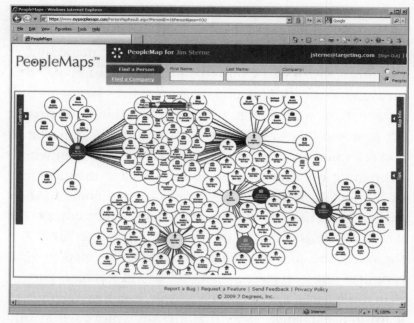

Figure 9.2   People-Map.com knows how you're connected and can show you.

How then, does a marketer make the most of this new mode of communication and measure whether the efforts are paying off?

Sticks and Stones

You will still have to craft a message—so people will know what to think initially. You will still address the masses—so there's still a need for mass media (television, radio, the press).

You will still propose an opinion that you'd like prospective customers to adopt. But how often you articulate your point of view will no longer be the most important metric. How many people buy from you will be predicated on what they have to say about you. Sticks and stones may break your bones but words can put you out of business.

Matt Langie, senior director of product marketing at Omniture, says, "We've started off the first decade of online measurement with how do I measure what's happening on my site? Now we see there's influence and things happening off your site that in some cases have far more importance and relevance to your business and effect on it than what's happening on your site. So, think about a manufacturer of product X. They may not have someone come to their site saying, 'Your product really changed my life for the worst or for the better or it's great or it's terrible. But there may be an entire blog community devoted to your products and services. Social media will become part of that town hall experience of people coming together to learn and exchange ideas that are far removed from the operations of your business, and your online business specifically."

Indeed, people who are using Twitter are finding it to be an excellent headline news feed. Not because the *Wall Street Journal*, the *New York Times*, and the *Washington Post* all tweet really well, but because of crowdsourcing the news. When a story breaks, they read tweets about it and click through to the stories.

That's going to happen to your product launch as well. Create a cool enough product, slogan, or game and you'll be retweeted into stardom.

While social media becomes more and more important from the standpoint of getting the word out, the impact of that word is still going to be measured by the number of people it drives to your web site, your store, and your wallet. The vast amount of information already available about on-site behavior must be married up with the social data flow in order to reap the most benefits. That's going to take some doing.

Enumeration Integration

So much data, so little time.

- ♦ Web behavioral data

- ♦ Customer satisfaction data

- ♦ Business outcome data

- ♦ Competitive data

- ♦ Social interaction data

- ♦ Financial data

- ♦ Demographic data

- ♦ Psychographic data

- ♦ Technographic data

If and when all of this can be dropped into the hopper and correlated, the ability to cater to individuals and send the right message to the right person at the right time becomes an absolute necessity.

Make no mistake, this is going to be painful. This is heavy lifting or, as the technical team likes to describe it, "nontrivial." In the words of David Weinberger, "The universe is analog, messy, complex and subject to many interpretations."

Companies like Unica (www.unica.com) and Teradata (www.teradata.com) are coming at the problem from the marketing management and the data management side, while companies like Omniture (www.omniture.com) are coming at it from the web analytics side, and those like Webtrends (www.webtrends.com) are coming at it from the best-of-breed, systems integration-through-sharing side.

But the data are messy. It's going to take time to collect, cleanse, synchronize, correlate, and gain insight from all of these sources, and while you're at it, new things are going to come along that will knock your socks off. Some are here already.

Yes, We Will Read Your Mind

That's not exactly right. More accurate would be: "We can already read your mind."

If you're like me, you were fascinated by Martin Lindstrom's book *Buyology: Truth and Lies About What We Buy* (Doubleday, 2008). He spent four years putting willing subjects into Functional Magnetic Resonance Imaging systems and watching which parts of their brains lit up when shown a variety of print ads, TV shows, and brand images. Wonderful stuff.

What follows, however, is the ultimate in social media metrics because it's the ultimate in human metrics. It is literally reading your mind—over the Internet—just by your visiting any web site that uses technology and analysis from NextStage Evolution (www.nextstageevolution.com).

You are now experiencing one of two reactions and likely both at the same time.

1. Jim has well and truly lost it.

2. This should be interesting.

Stick with me; I think you'll find #2 to be dominant by the end.

YOUR BRAIN IS UNIQUE

Each human brain starts out different from the rest based on its genetic inheritance. It then immediately proceeds to differentiate itself from others based on its real-world experience. Nature and Nurture. From nature it gets race, gender, and a penchant for some abilities over others. From nurture, just about everything else.

If you study the neural patterns in a brain, you can determine if the owner is male or female. There is a difference. (Vive la différence!)

The neural patterns in your brain are unique. Everybody—every brain—is different. But they share similarities in their differences. Male brains look more like male brains than they look like female brains. These similarities are recognizable enough to detect, for example, what language one speaks.

Brain-scanning technologies are great for measuring blood circulation and the amount of electricity flowing from one part of the brain to another. But they are insufficient for the sort of detection we're exploring here. For that, we need something more reliable, something more repeatable, something more sensitive. So we look to the human as a detection mechanism. Specifically, the individual human's use of a computer mouse when visiting a web site.

YOUR MOUSE TELEGRAPHS THE INNER YOU

Child development experts will tell you that a two-year-old child should be able to walk, handle stairs alone, sit in a chair, kick a ball, and turn the pages in a book. But they don't do any of those things as well as a three–year-old. Who doesn't do them as well as a four–year-old.

The child develops new skills because its brain recognizes situations and improves hand-eye coordination.

The neural pathways for walking, climbing, and kicking a ball are strengthened but not in a specific, rigorous way. They are reinforced in a haphazard, natural, human learning sort of a way.

That two–year-old does not handle a computer mouse as well as a three–year-old. It's not just practice, either. That ability is influenced by hand-eye coordination, of course, but also by cognitive skills, emotional development, intellectual capacity, and more.

Here's the key: How a person uses a web site (both mouse and keyboard) describes a certain neural pattern that can be compared with a database of others and classified by gender, age, and a lot more.

Using the latest research in neuroscience, linguistics, anthropology, and mathematics, NextStage Evolution is already offering a service to tell you the gender and age of your web site visitors. A double-blind test showed they were 99 percent accurate for gender and 97 percent accurate for age within three years. That's better than you or I could do on a stroll down Hollywood Boulevard.

Once you are comfortable with the idea of age and gender recognition, it's time to move on through individual identification to intent analysis. Using a matrix of Cognitive, Behavioral/Effective, and Motivational metrics, the movement of your mouse reveals a great deal.

The science behind this is serious and full of wonderfully multisyllabic terms. The NextStage web site reassures us that "Tests have been conducted in the areas of Gender Linguistic Modeling, LexicoStatistical Modeling, Memetic Recognition Modeling, Presentation Format Preference, Sensory to Teleology, Time Normalization Studies, Ungoaled Persistence."

Okay—let's get down to it. Here's how they describe their patented (yes) technology:

> *Evolution Technology is comprised of a series of modules or «engines» which have the ability to determine an individual's Learning styles, memorization methods, attentiveness, reactions to information and much more. Evolution technology does this by monitoring non-conscious psycho- and cognitive-motor behaviors during real time activities and is entirely passive. The system never asks individuals to fill out forms, to identify themselves, or go through an active recognition process. It can be adapted to any human-machine interface and our first efforts are in the Marketing and Web Analytics/Internet arena. Uses of this technology include Learning and training systems, marketing material optimization, ecommerce, intelligent-interactive systems (toys, cars, planes . . .), intruder detection, identification, detection of predatory behavior, detection of fabricated information (lying) and other security concerns.* (makingmarketingactionable .com/about-evolution-technology/)

It fact, the underlying technology can be used to analyze marketing materials like web sites and their appropriateness for the people who visit them.

But for now, let's just focus on a marketer's ability to hear the voice of the marketplace, measure the behavior of the web site visitor, and assess the intent of the customer. This four-dimensional picture should give hungry marketers more than enough information to unleash an ungodly tsunami of zombie-making advertising to create brain-wave-slaves who must buy now—Must buy now—Must Buy Now!

Are you completely freaked out yet?

NextStage is very well aware of this inherent dilemma and years ago laid out their principles for all to see (www.nextstagevolution.com/principles.cfm):

> *We know what our technology can do, probably better than anybody else out there. We know it can hurt people if used improperly, and we know there are people out there who wouldn't care if people are hurt so long as their profits keep going up.*
>
> *We're not like those people. Don't get us wrong. We enjoy profits as much as anybody.*
>
> *We just have certain ethical constraints on how we get those profits, and some of those ethical constraints are listed here as Principles. If you want to work for or with us you should know these principles exist and are adhered to in this company.*

Is that not enough to put your mind at ease? Are you still wondering where to buy that tinfoil beanie?

The funny thing about powerful tools in the hands of a marketing professional with deep pockets is that we live in an age of social media. The moment the public discovers that a company is trying to game the social system, they are immediately up in arms.

Companies that create fake fan blogs, pay bloggers under the table, and automate friending and following are exposed for the frauds that they are. The first time it happens in a social media situation, it's interesting that some Large Corporation deemed the cute little social networking tool worthy of their attention and the next Large Corporation is blasted for deceit. All others should quickly take note that online mendacity is punishable by a deep and abiding drop in brand affinity leveraged by tens of thousands of outraged individuals.

Not enough? Still worried that the NextStage technology in the wrong hands spells disaster? Wondering how on earth does this capability work in a world with such a tenuous hold on privacy? John McKean gave me an answer.

Customers Run the Show

John McKean is the executive director of the Center for Information Based Competition (www.informationmasters. com). I met him while doing some work on behalf of Teradata and realized at once that he had been working on something I have been hoping for, for more than a decade—true customer control.

After several conversations, I asked John to write us his perspective and approach for inclusion in this book and he acquiesced. (The following is reprinted by permission, copyright ©John McKean.)

> ***The Future of web measurement . . . the fatal current-state assumption . . . or Consumers as Information Integration Point . . . Next Generation of Web Empowerment . . . and Measurement***
> *Current thinking of how the social media/web will be measured in the future has one fatal flaw. It assumes that the Web's transformation of our current business model will continue on its current trajectory as will the relative incarnations of its measurement. It will not.*

The web's future transformation of our current consumer business models will not only eclipse the previous effects on current models but will drive a complete inversion of these consumer business models.

Our preoccupation with "current state" has placed us in a dangerously naïve position with our assumptions that the advancement of web analytics will continue with organizations as the point of information integration. It will not.

The next incarnation of the web will place the consumer squarely as the point of data integration.

If we consider our current state . . .

Organizations are already dangerously behind the consumer's ability to leverage the Web for online and offline information. This reality places an organization's relevancy at great risk. By the sheer law of markets and consumer behavior, consumer information integration will begin shifting from organizations to consumers . . . the complete reciprocal of our current business models. Why? The best place for the most relevant consumer information is the consumer and always has been.

The consumer just hasn't had a mature information enabler such as the web to facilitate this strategic information shift. The technology layer of this information enabler is now in place. The consumer is also the most efficient place for this information to reside from a macroeconomic, market, and consumer perspective. Most importantly, the consumer has the best knowledge regarding their future buying actions and verifying their buying intentions.

Currently, the vast proportion of innovation is happening on the "buy side" of consumer interactions. The "sell" side innovations are progressively being less and less. Within 10 years, consumers will be the sole integration point of their own information, and businesses will be operating in the complete reciprocal of their current customer management strategies and practices. This consumer information shift will have the historic and economic significance of the Industrial Revolution.

The seemingly fundamental transformational effects that the advent of Google, YouTube, eBay, and Facebook has had on the evolution from a centralized and structured system of business to one of conversation and collaboration between individuals will pale in comparison to a world in which the consumer [is] the point of information integration.

A world where consumers initiate each consumption activity/interaction, manage their own experience, and determine what information is collected, how it is used, and how it is disseminated.

The current-day equivalent would be our B2B business model relative to RFI's [Request For Information] except they will be issued by individuals to businesses, i.e., Personal RFI's. This business model will spawn an entire new industry for the "information machine" required to match the individual's request and potential suppliers or 3rd or 4th party service providers, i.e., information intermediaries. It will also give rise to an entire new system of protecting information privacy for managing this new information flow in both directions.

This new consumer information architecture will be a robust personal data ecosystem with dimensions of both analytical and operational data. It will consist of some premium forms of data with a basic [identity] set, i.e., the identity glue. These will . . . double the number of data flows of the current business models which will enable this personal data ecosystem. These will drive such dynamics for consumer buying requirements articulation and preferences pushed out via an XML-equivalent communication to accomplish activities such as offer access or suppression.

Other systems will be in place to control the deployment and broadcast of alerts, reminders, and notifications tied to measurement and analyses of offers and requirements. This architecture will all be published as an open standard (. . . to the API level) articulating such dimensions as search and offer comparison, defining such elements as availability, tradeoffs for convenience, levels of service, and definition of a knowledgeable, trusted information source.

The magnitude of market efficiencies that this creates is staggering. The sheer resources (time and money) that organizations invest to "guess" what to sell the consumer as oppose[d] to the consumer telling the organizations what they want to buy is immense. In this new paradigm, the consumer providing complete buying context completely eviscerates an organization's attempt at analytics against consumer segmentation in both the pre- and post-buying transaction. Current best-in-class consumer segmentation by organizations touts a 95%–98% failure rate. This failure percentage communicates to the consumer "We don't know you, We don't Respect you, and You're unimportant". Bottom line: You can't trust us.

The inefficient and ineffective B2C "dance" of target-and-manage now becomes a consumer-initiated dance (C2B) of Search, Find (engage), and Negotiate ... in complete relevancy and efficiency.

Worried about your brain pattern being sold to the highest bidder who wants it to sell you toothpaste? Worry not. From where I sit, the future is secure in your hands as a consumer. As a marketer, however, things are just starting to get interesting.

APPENDIX
Resources

Importance of Social Media

Do Friends Influence Purchases in a Social Network?

Harvard Business School Paper
In spite of the cultural and social revolution in the rise of social networking sites such as Facebook and MySpace (and in South Korea, Cyworld), the business viability of these sites remains in question. While many sites are attempting to follow Google and generate revenues from advertising, will advertising be effective? If friends influence the purchases of a user in a social network, it could potentially be a significant source of revenue for the sites and their corporate sponsors. Using a unique data set from Cyworld, this study empirically assesses if friends indeed influence purchases. The answer: It depends. Findings are relevant for social networking sites and large advertisers.

http://hbswk.hbs.edu/item/6185.html

Social Media Definitions

WEB ANALYTICS ASSOCIATION SOCIAL MEDIA STANDARDS

Interactive Advertising Bureau Social Media Ad Metrics Definitions

This document specifies standard definitions for Social Media Metrics. With the rapid growth seen in the Social Media space in recent years, many publishers and vendors are offering supplemental performance metrics to their clients as an additional way of gauging ad effectiveness. This document defines these supplemental metrics, in more detail, in an effort to stimulate growth by making the reporting of metrics for agencies and advertisers across multiple media partners more consistent. The IAB hopes that all players in the Social Media space will coalesce around these metrics to encourage growth through consistency.

http://www.webanalyticsassociation.org/?page=social-media-standards

Social Media Advertising Consortium

LEARN TO TALK SMAC

Every trade needs a standard vocabulary to refer to its environment, users, actions, products and results. Surprise, social media didn't have one! So we took the bull by the horns, collected over 200 terms that we'd seen or used, and then edited, sorted and defined the list. The result is documented here, on the SMAC Wiki. As our industry grows, we will continually review and add those terms that reach a critical mass of usage.

http://wiki.smac.org/

Measuring Social Media

CONVERSATION IMPACT: OGILVY'S SIMPLE, RESULTS-DRIVEN SOCIAL MEDIA MEASUREMENT MODEL FOR MARKETERS

With two-thirds of the world's Internet population now visiting a blog or social networking site, driving results through social media has become an important component of the marketing strategy. To help guide brands on social media spending decisions, Ogilvy's global social media marketing group, 360° Digital Influence, has developed and introduced a new business objective-driven model that provides a quantitative measurement framework for [social] media effectiveness—Conversation Impact.

http://insideraccess.ogilvypr.com/system/attachments/ 3/original/OPR_360DI_WhitePaper_Conversation_Impact_ FINAL.pdf

Zocalogroup's Measuring Digital Word of Mouth

PATRICK ROONEY, RYAN RASMUSSEN AND SUE FOGEL, PH.D., JULY 2009

What is really needed is a way to evaluate, measure, and track a brand's online presence multidimensionally; a measure that will show not only the quantity of conversation, but also quality; the level of interaction and the depth of message penetration and saturation.

http://www.zocalogroup.com/orange-papers/Measuring %20Digital%20Word%20of%20Mouth.pdf

Razorfish's Measuring Social Influence Marketing Report

Social Influence Marketing (SIM) is about employing social media and social influencers to achieve the marketing and business needs of an organization.

Social Influence Marketing is about recognizing, accounting, and tapping into the fact that as your potential consumer makes a purchasing decision, he or she is being influenced by different circles of people through conversations with them, both online and off. It is not enough to market to the consumer anymore; as a marketer you also have to market to each individual's social influencers throughout the marketing funnel.

As brands seek to *do* versus *push*, they're not going to differentiate between online and offline. And even more so than in the past, they'll want to measure what their brands do. So we've also looked at how trust works across the different platforms online and offline. With our partners TNS Cymfony and The Keller Fay Group, we've studied how brand sentiment varies by industry and by channel (online versus offline) to define what we refer to as a SIM Score— a single metric that every brand will need to index itself against on an ongoing basis.

http://fluent.razorfish.com/publication/?m=6540&l=1

Social Media Measurement Tools

Ongoing list of Companies that Measure Social Media

Jeremiah Owyang

I'm very interested in finding companies that can measure social media, not just blogs, not just podcasts, not just viral sites, but all social media.

http://www.web-strategist.com/blog/2006/11/25/
companies-that-measure-social-media-influence-brand/

ONLINE BRAND REPUTATION OR SOCIAL MEDIA LISTENING SOFTWARE—A REVIEW OF 26 TOOLS

Dave Chaffey

One of the defining features of 2009 for me personally was the power of Twitter to share ideas and tools with others. This post is a great example of this. I hope you find it useful. Please share your comments on which of these tools you have found effective or let us know about others that aren't on the list.

http://www.davechaffey.com/blog/online-pr/online-reputation-management-software/

Measurement Camp Tools For Measurement

The list of free measurement sites from MeasurementCamp II is on Delicious, using the tags "measurementcamp08" and "snapshot." The idea being that we collect a list of sites which can be used for free to create a snapshot of the activity levels of a piece of social media, to benchmark against.

http://measurementcamp.wikidot.com/tools-for-measurement

Social Media Metrics Discussions

BUSINESS EXCHANGE

http://bx.businessweek.com/social-media-analytics/
Socialmetrix.com

Social Media Resource Pages

ROYSITEPU'S POSTEROUS

A collection of valuable resources, tools, & advice specifically on the topics of social media measurement, monitoring, and ROI. You'll also find a handful of key social media statistics resources to put in your toolkit.

http://roysitepu.posterous.com/social-media-metrics-superlist-measurement-ro-1

Index

A

Acuvue Wink, 43
AddThis, 126
Advertising. *See also*
    Marketing
    attracting, 23–24
    blogging metrics, 22–27
    frequency, 17–18
    platforms, 16–17
    publishers selling, 25
Age recognition tools, 220
Allen, Woody, 115
American Customer
        Satisfaction Index
        (ACSI), 137–138
Analysis. *See also* Text
        analysis tools
    function, 3
    marketing, 12–13
    networks, 61–63
    prioritizing, 10
    understanding, 11–12
ANEW (Affective Norms
        English Words), 90
Application programming
        interfaces (APIs),
        113–114
Apps, 43–45, 49–50
Artificial intelligence
    function, 97
    human guidance,
        98–99
    machine learning tenant,
        93
Attensity, 97
Attributes, 22
Audiences. *See also*
        Customers
    brand recognition, 19–22
    citations, 55–56
    measurement, 42
    reaching
        definition, 16
        importance, 15
        platforms, 16–17
        reports, 28–29
    survey tools, 173–174
    Twitter, 51–52
    types
        fans, 53–54
        followers, 53
        readers, 52

    repeaters, 54–56
    subscribers, 53
Authority
    context and, 75
    impact, 70–74
    use, 69–70
Average Daily Feed
        Subscribers, 30
Awareness, 15
Axiom, 63

B

Baekdal, Thomas, 53
Bag-words approach,
        87–89, 94
Bazaarvoice, 79, 132
Benioff, Mark, 146
Bernoff, Josh, 180
Bernier, John, 153–155
Berra, Yogi, 4
Best Buy, 152–154
Bit.ly, 116
Blog readership, 29–31
Blog value index *a*, 24
Blogging
    metrics, 22–27
    opportunity costs, 27
    ROI, 24–25
Blogs. *See also* Posts
    brand mentions, 40–41
    fake, 222
    hubs, 56–57, 59
    humor and, 118–119
    Occam's Razor, 31
    rating, 96
    reach, cost, 184
    repeaters, 54–56
    spokes, 56–57, 59, 61–63
    subscriber counts, 27–29
    Technorati measure, 70
    Tweets *versus,* 55
    visitors, total number, 30
Brain
    development, 219–220
    imaging, 218
    neural patterns, 219
    scanning technologies,
        219
Brands
    apps and, 43
    blog mentions, 40–41
    recognition, 19–22

    tracking through, 176
    view through, 117–118
Brandsrecall, 22
BreakingPoint, 42
Business
    blogging metrics, 22–27
    desired outcomes,
        164–165
    key goals, 5–8
    satires, 118
*Buyology: Truth and Lies
        about What We Buy*
        (Lindstrom), 218
Buzz Up, 110
Buzzcom, 31
Buzzmetrics, 172

C

Calculators, 8–10
Cardie, Claire, 84
Careaga, Andrew, 108
Carroll, Dave, 140
Child development patterns,
        219–220
Citations, 55–56
Click-through rate (CTR),
        115
The Cluetrain Manifesto,
        124
Coca-Cola, 20
Comments. *See* Responses
Communication. *See*
        Conversations
Community
    health factors
        content, 177–178
        frameworks, 180–182
        liveliness, 179–180
        membership, 177
        responsiveness,
            178–179
        topic interaction, 179
        traffic, 177–178
    key indicators, 175–176
    manager's role, 175
    skills assessment, 182–184
Comparative measurement,
        114–115
Complaints
    focused grievances,
        139–140
    generic, 139